Statistical Significance Testing for Natural Language Processing

Synthesis Lectures on Human Language Technologies

Editor
Graeme Hirst, *University of Toronto*

Synthesis Lectures on Human Language Technologies is edited by Graeme Hirst of the University of Toronto. The series consists of 50- to 150-page monographs on topics relating to natural language processing, computational linguistics, information retrieval, and spoken language understanding. Emphasis is on important new techniques, on new applications, and on topics that combine two or more HLT subfields.

Statistical Significance Testing for Natural Language Processing
Rotem Dror, Lotem Peled-Cohen, Segev Shlomov, and Roi Reichart

ISBN: 978-3-031-01046-0 paperback
ISBN: 978-3-031-02174-9 ebook
ISBN: 978-3-031-00185-7 hardcover

DOI 10.1007/978-3-031-02174-9

A Publication in the Springer series
SYNTHESIS LECTURES ON ADVANCES IN AUTOMOTIVE TECHNOLOGY

Lecture #45
Series Editor: Graeme Hirst, *University of Toronto*
Series ISSN
Print 1947-4040   Electronic 1947-4059

Statistical Significance Testing for Natural Language Processing

Rotem Dror, Lotem Peled-Cohen, Segev Shlomov, and Roi Reichart

Technion – Israel Institute of Technology

SYNTHESIS LECTURES ON HUMAN LANGUAGE TECHNOLOGIES #45

ABSTRACT

Data-driven experimental analysis has become the main evaluation tool of Natural Language Processing (NLP) algorithms. In fact, in the last decade, it has become rare to see an NLP paper, particularly one that proposes a new algorithm, that does not include extensive experimental analysis, and the number of involved tasks, datasets, domains, and languages is constantly growing. This emphasis on empirical results highlights the role of statistical significance testing in NLP research: If we, as a community, rely on empirical evaluation to validate our hypotheses and reveal the correct language processing mechanisms, we better be sure that our results are not coincidental.

The goal of this book is to discuss the main aspects of statistical significance testing in NLP. Our guiding assumption throughout the book is that the basic question NLP researchers and engineers deal with is whether or not one algorithm can be considered better than another one. This question drives the field forward as it allows the constant progress of developing better technology for language processing challenges. In practice, researchers and engineers would like to draw the right conclusion from a limited set of experiments, and this conclusion should hold for other experiments with datasets they do not have at their disposal or that they cannot perform due to limited time and resources. The book hence discusses the opportunities and challenges in using statistical significance testing in NLP, from the point of view of experimental comparison between two algorithms. We cover topics such as choosing an appropriate significance test for the major NLP tasks, dealing with the unique aspects of significance testing for non-convex deep neural networks, accounting for a large number of comparisons between two NLP algorithms in a statistically valid manner (multiple hypothesis testing), and, finally, the unique challenges yielded by the nature of the data and practices of the field.

KEYWORDS

Natural Language Processing, statistics, statistical significance, hypothesis testing, algorithm comparison, deep neural network models, replicability analysis

Contents

Preface

The field of Natural Language Processing (NLP) has made substantial progress in the last two decades. This progress stems from multiple sources: the data revolution that has made abundant amounts of textual data from a variety of languages and linguistic domains available, the development of increasingly effective predictive statistical models, and the availability of hardware that can apply these models to large datasets. This dramatic improvement in the capabilities of NLP algorithms carries the potential for a great impact.

The extended reach of NLP algorithms has also resulted in NLP papers giving more and more emphasis to the experiment and result sections by showing comparisons between multiple algorithms on various datasets from different languages and domains. It can be safely argued that the ultimate test for the quality of an NLP algorithm is its performance on well-accepted datasets, sometimes referred to as "leader-boards". This emphasis on empirical results highlights the role of statistical significance testing in NLP research: If we rely on empirical evaluation to validate our hypotheses and reveal the correct language processing mechanisms, we better be sure that our results are not coincidental.

The goal of this book is to discuss the main aspects of statistical significance testing in NLP. Particularly, we aim to briefly summarize the main concepts so that they are readily available to the interested researcher, address the key challenges of hypothesis testing in the context of NLP tasks and data, and discuss open issues and the main directions for future work.

We start with two introductory chapters that present the basic concepts of statistical significance testing: Chapter 2 provides a brief presentation of the hypothesis testing framework, and Chapter 3 introduces common statistical significance tests. Then, Chapter 4 discusses the application of statistical significance testing to NLP. In Chapter 4, we assume that two algorithms are compared on a single dataset, based on a single output that each of them produces, and discuss the relevant significance tests for various NLP tasks and evaluation measures. The chapter puts an emphasis on the aspects in which NLP tasks and data differ from common examples in the statistical literature, e.g., the non–Gaussian distribution of the data and the dependence between the participating examples, e.g., sentences in the same corpus. This chapter, which extends our ACL 2018 paper [Dror et al, 2018], provides our recommended matching between NLP tasks with their evaluation measures and statistical significance tests.

The next two chapters relax two of the basic assumptions of Chapter 4: (a) that each of the compared algorithms produces a single output for each test example (e.g., a single parse tree for a given input sentence), and (b) that the comparison between the two algorithms is performed on a single dataset. Particularly, Chapter 5 addresses the comparison between two algorithms based on multiple solutions where each of them produces for a single dataset, while Chapter 6 addresses the comparison between two algorithms across several datasets.

The first challenge stems from the recent emergence of Deep Neural Networks (DNNs), which has made data-driven performance comparison much more complicated. This is because these models are non-deterministic due to their non-convex objective functions, complex hyper-parameter tuning process and training heuristics such as random dropouts, that are often applied in their implementation. Chapter 5, therefore, defines a framework for a statistically valid comparison between two DNNs based on multiple solutions each of them produces for a given dataset. The chapter summarizes previous attempts in the NLP literature to perform this comparison task and evaluates them in light of the proposed framework. Then, it presents a new comparison method that is better fitted to the pre-defined framework. This chapter is based on our ACL 2019 paper [Dror et al., 2019].

The second challenge is crucial for the efforts to extend the reach of NLP technology to multiple domains and languages. These well-justified efforts result in a large number of comparisons between algorithms, across corpora from a large number of languages and domains. The goal of this chapter is to provide the NLP community with a statistical analysis framework, termed Replicability Analysis, which will allow us to draw statistically sound conclusions in evaluation setups that involve multiple comparisons. The classical goal of replicability analysis is to examine the consistency of findings across studies in order to address the basic dogma of science, namely that a finding is more convincingly true if it is replicated in at least one more study [Heller et al., 2014, Patil et al., 2016]. We adapt this goal to NLP, where we wish to ascertain the superiority of one algorithm over another across multiple datasets, which may come from different languages, domains, and genres. This chapter is based on our TACL paper [Dror et al., 2017].

Finally, while this book aims to provide a basic framework for proper statistical significance testing in NLP research, it is by no means the final word on this topic. Indeed, Chapter 7 presents a list of open questions that are still to be addressed in future research. We hope that this book will contribute to the evaluation practices in our community and eventually to the development of more effective NLP technology.

INTENDED READERSHIP

The book is intended for researchers and practitioners in NLP who would like to analyze their experimental results in a statistically sound manner. Hence, we assume technical background in computer science and related areas such as statistics and probability, mostly at the undergraduate level. Moreover, while in Chapter 4 we discuss various NLP tasks and their proposed significance tests, our discussion of these tasks is quite shallow. Furthermore, when we analyze experimental results with NLP tasks in Chapters 5 and 6 we do not provide the details of the tasks because we assume the reader is familiar with the basic tasks of NLP. Despite these assumptions about the reader's background, we are trying as much as possible to be self-contained when it comes to statistical hypothesis testing and the derived concepts and methodology, as presenting these ideas to the NLP audience is a core objective of this book.

Further Reading   For broader and more in-depth reading on the fundamental concepts of statistics, we refer the reader to other existing resources such as Montgomery and Runger [2007] (which provides an engineering perspective) and Johnson and Bhattacharyya [2019]. For further reading on the topic of multiple comparisons in statistics, we recommend the book by Bretz et al. [2016] which demonstrates the basic concepts and provides examples with R code.

This book evolved from a series of conference and journal papers—Dror et al. [2017], Dror et al [2018], Dror et al. [2019]—which have been greatly expanded in order to form this book. First, we added background chapters that discuss the foundations of statistical hypothesis testing and provide the details of the statistical significance tests that we find most relevant for NLP. Then, we take the handbook approach and provide the pseudocode of the various methods discussed throughout the book, along with concrete recommendations and guidelines—our goal is to allow the practitioner to directly and easily implement the methods described in this book. Finally, in Chapter 7, we critically discuss the ideas presented in this book and point to challenges that are yet to be addressed in order to perform statistically sound analysis of NLP experimental results.

FOCUS OF THIS BOOK

This book is intended to be self-contained, presenting the framework of statistical hypothesis testing and its derived concepts and methodology in the context of NLP research. However, the main focus of the book is on this statistical framework and its application to the analysis of NLP experimental results, rather than on providing in-depth coverage of the NLP field.

Most of the book takes the handbook approach and aims to provide concrete solutions to practical problems. As such, it does not provide in-depth technical coverage of statistical hypothesis testing to a level that will allow the reader to propose alternative solutions to those proposed here, or to solve some of the open challenges we point to. Yet, our hope is that highlighting the challenges of statistically sound evaluation of NLP experiments, both those that already have decent solutions and those that are still open, will attract the attention of the community to these issues and facilitate future development of additional methods and techniques.

Rotem Dror, Lotem Peled-Cohen, Segev Shlomov, and Roi Reichart
April 2020

Acknowledgments

This book is an outcome of three years of exploration. The journey started with a course by Dr. Marina Bogomolov on multiple hypothesis testing, which was given in the fall of 2017 at the Faculty of Industrial Engineering and Management (IE&M) of the Technion. Marina, as well as Gili Baumer, her M.Sc. student and the tutor of the course at the time, were instrumental in the research that resulted in Chapter 6 of this book.

Many people commented on the ideas we discuss in the book, read drafts of the papers that were eventually extended into this book as well as versions of the book itself, and provided valuable feedback. Among these are David Azriel, Eustasio Del Barrio, Yuval Pinter, David Traum (who, as the program chair of ACL 2019, made a substantial contribution to the shaping of our ideas in Chapter 5), Or Zuk, and the members of the Natural Language Processing Group of the IE&M Faculty of the Technion: Reut Apel, Chen Badler, Eyal Ben David, Amichay Doitch, Ofer Givoli, Amir Feder, Ira Leviant, Rivka (Riki) Malka, Nadav Oved, Guy Rotman, Ram Yasdi, Yftah Ziser, and Dor Zohar.

The anonymous reviewers of the book and original papers provided detailed comments on various aspects of this work, from minor technical details to valuable suggestions on the structure, that dramatically improved its quality. Graeme Hirst, Michael Morgan, and Christine Kiilerich orchestrated the book-writing effort and provided valuable guidance.

Finally, we would like to thank the generous support of the Technion Graduate School. Rotem Dror has also been supported by a generous Google Ph.D. fellowship.

Needless to say that all the mistakes and shortcomings of the book are ours. Please let us know if you find any.

Rotem Dror, Lotem Peled-Cohen, Segev Shlomov, and Roi Reichart
April 2020

CHAPTER 1

Introduction

The field of Natural Language Processing (NLP) has made substantial progress in the last two decades. This progress stems from multiple reasons: the data revolution that has made abundant amounts of textual data from a variety of languages and linguistic domains available, the development of increasingly effective predictive statistical models, and the availability of hardware that can apply these models to large datasets. This dramatic improvement in the capabilities of NLP algorithms carry the potential for a great impact.

The extended reach of NLP algorithms has also resulted in NLP papers giving more and more emphasis to the experiment and result sections by showing comparisons between multiple algorithms on various datasets from different languages and domains. It can be safely argued that the ultimate test for the quality of an NLP algorithm is its performance on well-accepted datasets, sometimes referred to as "leader-boards". This emphasis on empirical results highlights the role of statistical significance testing in NLP research: If we rely on empirical evaluation to validate our hypotheses and reveal the correct language processing mechanisms, we better be sure that our results are not coincidental.

The goal of this book is to discuss the main aspects of statistical significance testing in NLP. Particularly, we aim to briefly summarize the main concepts so that they are readily available to the interested researcher, address the key challenges of hypothesis testing in the context of NLP tasks and data, and discuss open issues and the main directions for future work.

We start with two introductory chapters that present the basic concepts of statistical significance testing: Chapter 2 provides a brief presentation of the hypothesis testing framework and Chapter 3 introduces common statistical significance tests. Then, Chapter 4 discusses the application of statistical significance testing to NLP. In this chapter we assume that two algorithms are compared on a single dataset, based on a single output that each of them produces, and discuss the relevant significance tests for various NLP tasks and evaluation measures. The chapter puts an emphasis on the aspects in which NLP tasks and data differ from common examples in the statistical literature, e.g., the non-Gaussian distribution of the data and the dependence between the participating examples, e.g., sentences in the same corpus. This chapter, that extends our ACL 2018 paper [Dror et al, 2018], provides our recommended matching between NLP tasks with their evaluation measures and statistical significance tests.

The next two chapters relax two of the basic assumptions of Chapter 4: (a) that each of the compared algorithms produces a single output for each test example (e.g., a single parse tree for a given input sentence); and (b) that the comparison between the two algorithms is performed on a single dataset. Particularly, Chapter 5 addresses the comparison between two algorithms based on multiple solutions where each of them produces for a single dataset, while Chapter 6 addresses the comparison between two algorithms across several datasets.

The first challenge stems from the recent emergence of Deep Neural Networks (DNNs), which has made data-driven performance comparison much more complicated. This is because these models are non-deterministic due to their non-convex objective functions, complex hyper-parameter tuning process, and training heuristics such as random dropouts that are often applied in their implementation. Chapter 5 hence defines a framework for a statistically valid comparison between two DNNs based on multiple solutions each of them produces for a given dataset. The chapter summarizes previous attempts in the NLP literature to perform this comparison task and evaluates them in light of the proposed framework. Then, it presents a new comparison method that is better fitted to the pre-defined framework. This chapter is based on our ACL 2019 paper [Dror et al., 2019].

The second challenge is crucial for the efforts to extend the reach of NLP technology to multiple domains and languages. These well-justified efforts result in a large number of comparisons between algorithms, across corpora from a large number of languages and domains. The goal of this chapter is to provide the NLP community with a statistical analysis framework, termed Replicability Analysis, which will allow us to draw statistically sound conclusions in evaluation setups that involve multiple comparisons. The classical goal of replicability analysis is to examine the consistency of findings across studies in order to address the basic dogma of science, namely finding is more convincingly true if it is replicated in at least one more study [Heller et al., 2014, Patil et al., 2016]. We adapt this goal to NLP, where we wish to ascertain the superiority of one algorithm over another across multiple datasets, which may come from different languages, domains, and genres. This chapter is based on our TACL paper [Dror et al., 2017].

Finally, while this book aims to provide a basic framework for proper statistical significance testing in NLP research, it is by no means the final word on this topic. Indeed, Chapter 7 presents a list of open questions that are still to be addressed in future research. We hope that this book will contribute to the evaluation practices in our community and eventually to the development of more effective NLP technology.

CHAPTER 2

Statistical Hypothesis Testing

We begin with a definition of the statistical hypothesis testing framework. This fundamental framework will then allow us to discuss statistical significance tests (Chapter 3) and later on their application to experimental research in NLP.

A statistical hypothesis is defined as an hypothesis that is testable by observing and analyzing a process modeled by a set of random variables. In the basic setting, two datasets are compared and a hypothesis is proposed for the statistical relationship between them. This hypothesis is usually suggested as an alternative to an ideal null hypothesis that (often) proposes no relationship between two datasets. If the relationship between the datasets seems unlikely under the null hypothesis according to a threshold probability—the significance level—the null hypothesis will be rejected.

In order to distinguish between the null hypothesis and the alternative hypothesis, we consider two conceptual types of errors. The first type of error occurs when the null hypothesis is wrongly rejected while the second occurs when we wrongfully do not reject the null hypothesis. These two types of errors are known as *type* I and *type* II errors, and we will further elaborate on them later on.

In empirical machine learning research in general, and in the NLP community in particular, we would often like to prove the superiority of one algorithm over the other, and present this superiority in terms of a statistically significant improvement according to an evaluation metric, such as accuracy or F-score.[1] Therefore, we begin by formulating a general hypothesis testing framework for the comparison between two algorithms. This is the common type of hypothesis testing framework applied in NLP, and its detailed formulation will help us develop our ideas.

2.1 HYPOTHESIS TESTING

We wish to compare two algorithms, A and B. As an example, let us consider a comparison between two machine translation (MT) algorithms: phrase-based MT (such as the Moses MT system [Koehn et al., 2007]) vs. an LSTM Neural Encoder-decoder Network (e.g., the model described in Cho et al. [2014]). In order to compare between the two algorithms, we would experiment with several different parallel corpora. Let X be the set of such corpora, i.e., a collection of datasets $X = \{X^1, X^2, \ldots, X^N\}$, where each data set X^i is comprised of sentence pairs, one from the source language and one from the target language. That is, for all

---

[1]In this book we use the terms evaluation metric and evaluation measure interchangeably.

$i \in \{1, \ldots, N\}$, $X^i = \{x_{i,1}, \ldots, x_{i,n_i}\}$, where $x_{i,j}$ is a source language sentence and its translation.

The difference in performance between the two algorithms is measured with one or more evaluation metrics. In our example, when evaluating the performance of machine translation systems, we may use several evaluation measures to assess the quality of translation from various angles. For example, we would probably like our MT system to provide an accurate translation but we may also want to encourage creativity and linguistic richness, and prefer systems that do not excessively repeat the same words and phrases. Accordingly, we would evaluate it using two vastly used different metrics: BLEU [Papineni et al., 2002] and PINC [Chen et al., 2011]. We denote our set of metrics as $\mathcal{M} = \{\mathcal{M}_1, \ldots, \mathcal{M}_m\}$.[2]

So far, we have our two MT algorithms A and B, trained and evaluated on a set of metrics $\mathcal{M} = \{\mathcal{M}_1, \ldots, \mathcal{M}_m\}$. We denote with $\mathcal{M}_j(ALG, X^i)$ the value of the measure $\mathcal{M}_j$ when algorithm ALG is applied to the dataset X^i. Without loss of generality, we assume that higher values of the measure are better.

We define the difference in performance between two algorithms, A and B, according to the measure $\mathcal{M}_j$ on the dataset X^i as:

$$\delta_j\left(X^i\right) = \mathcal{M}_j\left(A, X^i\right) - \mathcal{M}_j\left(B, X^i\right). \tag{2.1}$$

Finally, using this notation we formulate the following statistical hypothesis testing problem:

$$\begin{aligned} H_{0i}(j) &: \delta_j\left(X^i\right) \leq 0 \\ H_{1i}(j) &: \delta_j\left(X^i\right) > 0. \end{aligned} \tag{2.2}$$

The goal of testing the above hypotheses is to determine if algorithm A is significantly better than algorithm B on the dataset X^i using the evaluation measure $\mathcal{M}_j$. In our example, this translates to the following question: "Is the LSTM-based MT system better than the Phrase-based one on the Wikipedia parallel corpus when considering the BLEU metric?"

If we strive to show that the LSTM is superior to the phrase-based system (in the specific setup of the Wikipedia Corpus and the BLEU metric), we would need to provide statistically valid evidence. Our hypotheses can be described as follows: The (somewhat pessimistic) null hypothesis would state that there is no significant performance difference between the LSTM and the phrase-based system, or that the latter performs even better, while the alternative hypothesis would state that the LSTM performs significantly better.

More generally, in our formulation the null hypothesis, H_0, states that there is no difference between the performance of algorithm A and algorithm B, or that B performs better. This hypothesis is tested vs. the alternative statement, H_1—that A is superior. If the statistical test results in rejecting the null hypothesis, one concludes that A outperforms B in this setup— i.e., on dataset X^i with respect to the evaluation metric $\mathcal{M}_j$. Otherwise, there is not enough

---

[2]To keep the discussion concise, throughout this book we assume that only one evaluation measure is used. Our framework can be easily extended to deal with multiple measures.

evidence in the data to make the conclusion of rejecting the null hypothesis. In this case, it is uncustomary to claim that we accept the null hypothesis, since the null hypothesis is the starting point, and by posing an alternative hypothesis we try to challenge the idealized state.

Naturally, we could be wrong in our conclusion. Our specific experiments may show that the LSTM outperforms the phrase-based system in a certain setup, but this does not necessarily reflect the true nature of things. Let us now properly define the two types of errors that we may encounter in our hypothesis test.

- Type I error—rejection of the null hypothesis when it is true, i.e., there is no difference in performance between the two algorithms. For example, concluding that the LSTM is superior to the phrase-based system in the explored setting when, in fact, that is not the case in general.

- Type II error—non-rejection of the null hypothesis when the alternative hypothesis is true. For example, missing the fact that the LSTM is in fact superior to the phrase-based system.

Knowing which one of the hypotheses is correct with full certainty is practically impossible, as that would require us to create a sample of all possible scenarios, i.e., observe the complete data generating distribution. Therefore, in practice, we can never know which one of the two algorithms is superior, and so the statistical significance testing framework actually strives to minimize the probability of type I and type II errors. We will touch on this in the following section.

Note, however, that reducing the probability of one of the errors may cause an increase of the probability of the other. The classical approach to hypothesis testing is to find a test that guarantees that the probability of making a type I error is upper bounded by a predefined constant α—the *significance level* of the test—while keeping the probability of a type II error as low as possible. The last is also referred to as designing a test that is as *statistically powerful* as possible.

A statistical test is called *valid* if it controls a certain type I error criterion, i.e., it guarantees to bound the error criterion by a predefined constant. By this definition, however, high validity can be obtained by never rejecting any null hypothesis. Hence, the quality of a statistical test is measured not only by its validity, but also by its *power*: the probability that it would in fact reject a false null hypothesis. This probability is called the statistical power of the test. In general, we wish to design tests that are both valid and powerful.

In the following section we will introduce the concept of *p-value*, a statistical instrument that allows us to test whether or not the null hypothesis holds, based on a data sample that is available.

2.2   P-VALUE IN THE WORLD OF NLP

We will now discuss a practical approach for deciding whether or not to reject the null hypothesis. We focus on the setup where the performance of two algorithms, A and B, on a dataset X, is compared using an evaluation measure $\mathcal{M}$. Let us denote with $\mathcal{M}(ALG, X)$ the value of the evaluation measure $\mathcal{M}$ when algorithm ALG is applied to the dataset X. Without loss of generality, we assume that higher values of the measure are better. We define the difference in performance between the two algorithms according to the measure $\mathcal{M}$ on the dataset X as:

$$\delta(X) = \mathcal{M}(A, X) - \mathcal{M}(B, X). \tag{2.3}$$

In our example, A could be the LSTM and B the phrase-based MT system, and $\mathcal{M}$ could be the BLEU metric. According to Equation (2.3), $\delta(X)$ would be the difference in performance between our two MT algorithms with respect to the BLEU metric. We would like to test whether $\delta(X) > 0$, which would indicate a higher BLEU score (i.e., better performance) for the LSTM. However, we would also like to assess whether this result is likely to happen again in a new experiment, or whether the current experiment does not reflect the actual relationship between the algorithms.

We will refer to $\delta(X)$ as our *test statistic*—a quantity derived from the experiment and used for the statistical hypothesis testing. Using this notation we formulate the following statistical hypothesis testing problem[3]:

$$\begin{aligned} H_0 &: \delta(X) \leq 0 \\ H_1 &: \delta(X) > 0. \end{aligned} \tag{2.4}$$

The null hypothesis, H_0, is that $\delta(X)$ is smaller than or equal to zero, meaning that algorithm B is better than A, or that B is as good as A. In contrast, the alternative hypothesis, H_1, is that there is in fact a difference in performance and that algorithm A is superior. In order to decide whether or not to reject the null hypothesis, we can ask the following question.

> Considering the test statistic that we chose and its distribution under the null hypothesis, how likely would it be to encounter the $\delta(X)$ value that we have observed in our test, given that the null hypothesis is indeed correct?

After all, if $\delta(X)$ is a very large number, then algorithm A strongly outperformed algorithm B, and that would be unlikely under the hypothesis that algorithm B is better. To answer this question we will need to compute a probability term where $\delta(X)$ is a random variable, which requires some prior knowledge regarding its distribution under the null hypothesis—we will discuss this further later on this book. We therefore phrase our decision in terms of the probability of observing the $\delta_{observed}$ value if the null hypothesis was in fact true. This probability is exactly the *p*-value of the test.

---

[3]For simplicity we consider a one-sided hypothesis, it can be easily reformulated as a two-sided hypothesis.

The p-value is defined as the probability, under the null hypothesis H_0, of obtaining a result equal to or even more extreme than what was actually observed. For the hypothesis testing framework defined here, the p-value is defined as:

$$\Pr\left(\delta(X) \geq \delta_{observed} \mid H_0 \text{ is True}\right), \tag{2.5}$$

where $\delta_{observed}$ is the performance difference between the algorithms (according to $\mathcal{M}$) when they are applied to X. Going back to our example, we could describe the p-value as the probability that the LSTM shows such stronger performance in this setting (i.e., to observe such a $\delta_{observed}$) when the phrase-based MT system is actually a better model. If $\delta_{observed}$ is small, meaning the LSTM's BLEU score is only slightly better than that of the phrase-based system, it may very well be a statistical "fluke", such that if we were to repeat the experiment with a slightly different dataset from the same distribution we could probably encounter the opposite result of the phrase-based MT performing better. However, as $\delta_{observed}$ increases, the probability of encountering such values under the assumption that the phrase-based MT system is better becomes smaller and smaller.

The smaller the p-value, the stronger is the indication that the observed outcome is unlikely under the null hypothesis, H_0. In order to decide whether H_0 should be rejected, the researcher should pre-define an arbitrary, fixed threshold value α, a.k.a *the significance level*. Only if p-value $< \alpha$ then the null hypothesis is rejected.

For example, let us say that the probability to encounter a difference of 10 points between *BLEU(LSTM)* and *BLEU (phrase-based)* under the assumption that the phrase-based MT system is better, is 0.05. For a significance level of 0.1 we would reject the null hypothesis, since p-value $< \alpha$. For a significance level of 0.03 we would not reject the null hypothesis. A lower α is a stronger demand, equivalent to saying "We need to see a stronger, more extreme improvement in the LSTM in order to determine that it is a superior model. We want to see such a strong improvement (such a large $\delta_{observed}$), that would only have a probability of 0.03 or less under the null hypothesis."

How should we choose an α? As noted above, it is impossible to actually know which hypothesis is correct, H_0 or H_1, and hence we can only strive to minimize the probability of choosing the wrong hypothesis. A small α ensures that we do not reject the null hypothesis easily, but it may also cause us to not reject the null hypothesis when we should. More technically, a small α yields a lower probability of a type I error and a higher probability of a type II error. A common practice is to choose an α that guarantees that the probability of making a type I error is upper bounded by a pre-defined desired value, while achieving the highest possible power, i.e., the lowest possible probability of making a type II error. Popular α values in the literature are 0.05 and 0.01.

CHAPTER 3

Statistical Significance Tests

In this book, we are interested in the process of comparing performance of different NLP algorithms in a statistically sound manner. How is this goal related to the calculation of the p-value? Well, calculating the p-value is inextricably linked to statistical significance testing, as we will attempt to explain next. Recall the definition of $\delta(X)$ in Equation (2.3). $\delta(X)$ is our test statistic for the hypothesis test defined in Equation (2.3).

$\delta(X)$ is computed based on X, a specific data sample. In general, one can claim that if our data sample is representative of the data population, extreme values of $\delta(X)$ (either negative or positive) are less likely. In other words, the far left and right tails of the $\delta(X)$ distribution curve represent the unlikely events in which $\delta(X)$ obtains extreme values. What is the chance, given the null hypothesis is true, to have our $\delta(X)$ value land in those extreme tails? That probability is exactly the p-value obtained in the statistical test.

So, we now know that the probability of obtaining a $\delta(X)$ this high (or higher) is very low under the null hypothesis. Therefore, is the null hypothesis likely given this $\delta(X)$? Well, the answer is, most likely, no. It is much more likely that the performance of algorithm A is better. To summarize, because the probability of seeing such a $\delta(X)$ under the null hypothesis (i.e., seeing such a p-value) is very low ($< \alpha$), we reject the null hypothesis and conclude that there is a statistically significant difference between the performance of the two algorithms. This shows that statistical significance tests and the calculation of the p-value are parallel tools that help quantify the likelihood of the observed results under the null hypothesis.

In this chapter we move from describing the general framework of statistical significance testing to the specific considerations involved in the selection of a statistical significance test for an NLP application. We shall define the difference between parametric and nonparametric tests, and explore another important characteristic of the sample of scores that we work with, one that is highly critical for the design of a valid statistical test. We will present prominent tests useful for NLP setups, and conclude our discussion by providing a simple decision tree that aims to guide the process of selecting a significance test.

3.1 PRELIMINARIES

We previously presented an example of using the statistical significance testing framework for deciding between an LSTM and a phrase-based MT system, based on a certain dataset and evaluation metric, BLEU in our example. We defined our test statistic $\delta(X)$ as the difference in BLEU score between the two algorithms, and wanted to compute the p-value, i.e., the probability to observe such a $\delta(X)$ under the null hypothesis. But wait, how can we calculate this probability without knowing the distribution of $\delta(X)$ under the null hypothesis? Could we possibly choose a test statistic about which we have solid prior knowledge?

A major consideration in the selection of a statistical significance test is the distribution of the test statistic, $\delta(X)$, under the null hypothesis. If the distribution of $\delta(X)$ is known, then the suitable test will come from the family of *parametric tests*, that uses $\delta(X)$'s distribution under the null hypothesis in order to obtain statistically powerful results, i.e., have small probability of making a type II error. If the distribution under the null hypothesis is unknown then any assumption made by a test may lead to erroneous conclusions and hence we have to back off to *nonparametric tests* that do not make any such assumptions. While nonparametric tests may be less powerful than their parametric counterparts, they do not make unjustified assumptions and are hence statistically sound even when the test statistic distribution is unknown.

How can one know the test statistic distribution under the null hypothesis? One common tool is the Central Limit Theorem (CLT) which establishes that, in most situations, when independent random variables are added, their properly normalized sum tends toward a normal distribution even if the original variables themselves are not normally distributed. Hence, statistical significance tests defined over the mean of observations (e.g., the unlabeled attachment score, values of the parse trees of the test set sentences), often assume that this average is normally distributed after proper normalization.

Let us elaborate on this. Recall the definition of the test statistic $\delta(X)$ from Equation (2.3). In a dependency parsing example $\mathcal{M}(A, X)$ can be, for example, the unlabeled attachment score (UAS) for the parser of Kiperwasser and Goldberg [2016] (K&G) and $\mathcal{M}(B, X)$ can be the UAS score of the TurboParser [Martins et al., 2013]. Following the NLP literature, the test-set X is comprised of multiple sentences, and the metric $\mathcal{M}$ is calculated as the average score over all words in the test-set sentences. Hence, according to the CLT, the distribution of both $\mathcal{M}(A, X)$ and $\mathcal{M}(B, X)$ can be approximated by the normal distribution. Since $\delta(X)$ is defined as the difference between two variables with a normal distribution, it can also be assumed to have a normal distribution, which will make it easy for us to compute probabilities for its different possible values.

Unfortunately, in order to use the CLT, one is required to assume independence between the observations in the sample (test-set), and this independence assumption often does not hold in NLP setups. For example, a dependency parsing test-set (e.g., The WSJ Penn Treebank, Section 23 Marcus et al. [1993]) often consists of subsets of sentences taken from the same article, and many sentences in the Europarl parallel corpus [Koehn, 2005] are taken from the same parliament discussion. Later on in this book we will discuss this fundamental problem, and list it as one of the open issues to be considered in the context of statistical hypothesis testing in NLP.

If we cannot use the CLT in order to assume a normal distribution for the test statistic, we could potentially apply tests designed to evaluate the distribution of a sample of observations. For example, the Shapiro–Wilk test [Shapiro and Wilk, 1965] tests the null hypothesis that a sample comes from a normally distributed population, the Kolmogorov–Smirnov test quantifies the distance between the empirical cumulative distribution function of the sample and the cumulative distribution function of a reference distribution, and the Anderson-Darling test [Anderson and Darling, 1954] tests whether a given sample of data is drawn from a given probability distribution. As we will show later, there are other heuristics that are used in practice but are usually not mentioned in research papers.

To summarize the above discussion:

- Parametric tests—assume that we have complete knowledge regarding our test statistic's distribution under the null hypothesis. If we indeed have this knowledge, parametric tests can utilize it to ensure a low probability of making a type II error. However, if the distribution is unknown, then any assumptions made by such a test may lead to erroneous conclusions.

- Nonparametric tests—do not require the test statistic's distribution under the null hypothesis to be known or assumed. Nonparametric tests may be less powerful than their parametric counterparts as they do not make any assumptions about the test statistic distribution and are hence statistically sound even when the test statistic distribution is unknown.

In ensuring that we choose the appropriate statistical tool, we need not only to decide between a parametric and a nonparametric test, but should also consider another important quality of our dataset. Many statistical tests require an assumption of independence between the two populations (the test-set scores of the two algorithms in our case), and the following subtle point is often brushed aside: are the two populations that we are comparing between truly independent, or are they related to one another? Can we regard to samples that represent a state of "before" and "after" as independent? Or yet another example, from the world of NLP, can we regard as independent the scores of two different algorithms applied on the same sentence?

These above are examples of *paired samples*—samples in which a natural coupling occurs. In a dataset of paired samples (often called dependent samples), each data point in one sample is uniquely paired to a data point in the other sample. Paired samples can be before/after samples, in which a metric is computed before and after a certain action. Alternatively, they could be matched samples, in which individuals are matched on some characteristic such as age or gender. In general, paired samples appear in any circumstance in which each data point in one sample is directly matched to a data point in the other sample.

As opposed to the case of paired samples, sometimes we have *independent samples*, consisting of unrelated data points. Such independent samples can be obtained simply by randomly sampling from two different populations. A more realistic case in the world of medical experiments where two separate treatment groups (often a treatment group and a placebo group) are randomly created, without first matching the subjects.

Algorithm 3.1 Statistical Hypothesis Testing Process with Critical Regions

---

Input : H_0 the null hypothesis, H_1 the alternative hypothesis, α the significance level.
Output : Decision to either reject the null hypothesis in favor of the alternative or not reject it.

1: $O = \{\emptyset\}$—list of observations.
2: $O \leftarrow$ Perform experiment to test the hypotheses.
3: Decide which statistical test is appropriate.
4: Calculate the observed test statistic $T(O)$.
5: Derive the distribution of the test statistic under the null hypothesis H_0.
6: Calculate the *critical region*—the possible values of T for which the null hypothesis is rejected. The probability of the critical region under the distribution of the test statistic under the null hypothesis is α.
7: Reject the null hypothesis H_0 in favor of the alternative hypothesis H_1 if the observed test statistic $T(O)$ is in the critical region.

Algorithm 3.2 Statistical Hypothesis Testing Process with p-value

---

Input : H_0 the null hypothesis, H_1 the alternative hypothesis, α the significance level.
Output : Decision to either reject the null hypothesis in favor of the alternative or not reject it
Notice: steps 1–5 are the same as in Algorithm 3.1.

6: Calculate the p-value—the probability, under the null hypothesis H_0, of observing a test statistic at least as extreme as that which was observed.
7: Reject the null hypothesis H_0 in favor of the alternative hypothesis H_1 if and only if the p-value is less than (or equal to) α.

The notion of paired vs. independent samples is crucial in NLP. Oftentimes we are comparing between several algorithms on the same dataset and hence paired tests are more common. In what follows, we survey prominent parametric and nonparametric tests, emphasizing the paired setup. In addition, Algorithms 3.1 and 3.2 display a pseudo code of the general testing process that is applied when testing for statistical significance. The two processes are equivalent.

3.2   PARAMETRIC TESTS

As previously defined, parametric tests are statistical significance tests that assume prior knowledge regarding the test statistic's distribution under the null hypothesis. When using such tests, we utilize the test statistic's assumed distribution in order to ensure a bound on the type I error

Algorithm 3.3 The Paired Z-test

Input : Paired samples $\{x_i\}$, σ—standard deviation of the paired differences.
Output : p—the p-value.
Notations : n sample size.

1: Calculate the mean of the paired differences—$\bar{X} = \frac{1}{n} \sum_{i=1}^{n} x_i$.
2: Calculate the test statistic—$z = \frac{\bar{X}}{\sigma/\sqrt{n}}$.
3: Calculate $p = P(Z \geq z)$ where $Z \sim N(0, 1)$.

and a low probability of making a type II error. We will now elaborate on several prominent parametric tests that are suitable for the setup of paired samples.

We begin with tests that are highly relevant to NLP setups, accounting for cases where the metric values come from a normal distribution. Example relevant NLP metrics are sentence level accuracy, recall, unlabeled attachment score (UAS) and labeled attachment score (LAS) [Yeh, 2000].

Paired Z-test   In this test, the sample is assumed to be normally distributed and the standard deviation of the population is known. This test is used to validate the hypothesis that the sample drawn belongs to the same population through checking if the sample mean is the same as the population mean. This test is not very applicable in NLP since the population standard deviation is rarely known, but we define it here for completion. In addition, the statistical test which is used to validate the same hypothesis without the assumption on the known standard deviation in one of the most commonly used tests in NLP, the t-test which is described next. The Z-test is defined in Algorithm 3.3.

Paired Student's t-test   This test aims to assess whether the population means of two sets of measurements differ from each other, and is based on the assumption that both samples come from a normal distribution [Fisher, 1937]. The calculations of the test statistic and the p-value for this test are shown in Algorithm 3.4.

Since this test assumes a normal distribution and is computed over population means, one may argue that based on the Central Limit Theorem (CLT) it can be applied to compare between any large enough measurement sets; however, in NLP setups the test examples (e.g., sentences from the same document) are often dependent, violating the independence assumption of CLT.

In practice, t-test is often applied with evaluation measures such as accuracy, UAS and LAS, that compute the mean number of correct predictions per input example. When comparing two dependency parsers, for example, we can apply the test to check if the averaged difference of their UAS scores is significantly larger than zero, which can serve as an indication that one parser is better than the other. Using t-test with such metrics can be justified based on CLT.

Algorithm 3.4 The Paired Sample t-test

Input : Paired samples.

Output : p—the p-value.

Notations : D differences between two paired samples, d_i the ith observation in D, n the sample size, $\bar{d}$ the sample mean of the differences, $\hat{\sigma}$ the sample standard deviation of the differences, T the critical value of a t-distribution with $n - 1$ degrees of freedom, t the t-statistic (t-test statistic) for a paired sample t-test.

1: Calculate the sample mean—$\bar{d} = \frac{1}{n} \sum_{i=1}^{n} d_i$.

2: Calculate the sample standard deviation—$\hat{\sigma} = \sqrt{\frac{1}{n-1} \left(\sum_{i=1}^{n} d_i^2 - (\sum_{i=1}^{n} d_i)^2 \right)}$.

3: Calculate the test statistic—$t = \frac{\bar{d}}{\hat{\sigma}/\sqrt{n}}$.

4: Find the p-value in the t-distribution table, using the predefined significance level and $n - 1$ degrees of freedom.

That is, accuracy measures in structured tasks tend to be normally distributed when the number of individual predictions (e.g., number of words in a sentence when considering sentence-level UAS) is large enough.

One case where it is theoretically justified to employ the t-test is described in Sethuraman [1963]. The authors prove that for large enough data, the sampling distribution of a certain function of the Pearson's correlation coefficient follows the Student's t-distribution with $n - 2$ degrees of freedom, where n is the number of samples. With the recent surge in word similarity research with word embedding models, this result is of importance to our community. An example where this property is used can be found in Preoţiuc-Pietro et al. [2017].

For other evaluation measures, such as F-score, BLEU, METEOR, and ROUGE that do not compute means, the common practice is to assume that they are **not normally distributed** [Berg-Kirkpatrick et al., 2012, Yeh, 2000]. We believe that in these cases it is probably best to rely on the normality tests previously discussed when deciding whether or not to employ the t-test.

ANOVA   stands for *Analysis of Variance*. It is a process used to test hypotheses on sample means when dealing with several populations. ANOVA is a powerful statistical technique, its strength resides in testing the hypothesis that the means of two (or more) sets are equal, under the assumption that the sampled populations are normally distributed. The algorithm for a one-way ANOVA appears in Algorithm 3.5

For example, in Leviant and Reichart [2015], the authors explored whether the human similarity scores for word pairs differ across judgment languages, i.e., the languages in which the word pairs are presented to the human annotators. The authors translated two prominent

Algorithm 3.5 The One-way ANOVA

Input : $\{y_{ij}\}$—the ith observation ($i = 1, \ldots, n_j$) of the jth factor ($j = 1, \ldots, k$).
Output : p—the p-value.
Notations : F the test statistic that follows $F_{(k-1, n-1)}$-distribution.

1: Calculate $SS_{treatment} = \sum_{j=1}^{k} n_j (\bar{y}_j - \bar{y})^2$.
2: Calculate $SS_{error} = \sum_{j=1}^{k} \sum_{i=1}^{n_j} (y_{ij} - \bar{y}_j)^2$.
3: Calculate the test statistic—$F = \frac{SS_{treatment}/(k-1)}{SS_{error}/(n-k)}$.
4: Calculate $p = P(F > F_{(k-1, n-1, \alpha)})$ #for a one-sided hypothesis.

evaluation sets to four languages and collected word pair similarity scores for each dataset from annotators fluent in its language. In this experiment, the annotator language is referred to as a factor, according to the ANOVA model.

What is a factor? A factor is an independent treatment variable whose settings (values) are controlled and varied by the experimenter. The intensity setting of a factor is the level. Levels may be integer numbers or, in many cases, simply "present" or "not present" ("0" or "1").

The one-way ANOVA: in the experiment above, there is only one factor, language, and the analysis of variance that we will be using to analyze the effect of judgment language is called a one-way or one-factor ANOVA. The two-way ANOVA: we could have opted to also study the effect of level of education of annotators on the scores they give in the task. In this case there would be two factors: judgment language and education level. Here, we speak of a two-way or two-factor ANOVA. Furthermore, we may be interested in a third factor, the effect of age of annotators. Now we deal with a three-way or three-factor ANOVA. In each of these ANOVA techniques we test a variety of hypotheses of equality of means or average responses when the factors are varied.

The hypotheses that can be tested with ANOVA are dependent on the number of factors. First consider the one-way ANOVA; the null hypothesis is: there is no difference in the population means of the different levels of factor A (the only factor). The alternative hypothesis is: the means are different. For the two-way ANOVA, the possible null hypotheses are: There is no difference in the means of factor A, there is no difference in the means of factor B, there is no interaction between factor A and B. The alternative hypothesis for cases 1 and 2 is: the means are not equal; The alternative hypothesis for case 3 is: there is an interaction between A and B.

For the three-way ANOVA, the main effects are factors A, B, and C, and the two-factor interactions are AB, AC, and BC. There is also a three-factor interaction, ABC. For each of the seven cases the null hypothesis is the same: there is no difference between the means, and the alternative hypothesis is that the means are not equal.

The *n*-way ANOVA: In general, the number of main effects and interactions can be found by the following expression: $N = (n_0) + (n_1) + (n_2) + \ldots + (n_n)$. The first right-hand side term (n_0) is for the overall mean, and is always 1. The second term is for the number of main effects. The third term is for the number of two-factor interactions, and so on. The last term is for the *n*-factor interaction and is always 1.

Pearson's r-test   When working with paired samples, Pearson's r-test is often relevant. The Pearson correlation coefficient measures the strength of the linear relationship between two numeric variables. This coefficient is one of several correlation coefficients that quantify the relationship between two ordinal variables, another popular example is Spearman's rank correlation coefficient. The value of such correlation coefficients ranges from -1 to 1, where both extremes represent a perfect linear correlation, that is, both numeric variables grow or diminish together. The 0 value, in contrast, stands for no linear correlation.

In NLP, Pearson correlation can be calculated when wanting to prove a correlation or equivalency between algorithms, tasks or datasets. For example, Wieting and Gimpel [2017] used Pearson correlation to demonstrate similar performance between different types of LSTM networks in the task of sentence similarity.

The coefficient is calculated as follows:

$$r_{xy} = \frac{\sum_{i=1}^{n}(x_i - \bar{x})(y_i - \bar{y})}{\sqrt{\sum_{i=1}^{n}(x_i - \bar{x})^2}\sqrt{\sum_{i=1}^{n}(y_i - \bar{y})^2}}, \tag{3.1}$$

where $\bar{x}$ and $\bar{y}$ represent the mean of the samples. If the pairs come from an uncorrelated bivariate normal distribution, the sampling distribution of a certain function of Pearson's correlation coefficient follows the Student's t-distribution with $n - 2$ degrees of freedom. Specifically, if the underlying variables have a bi-variate normal distribution, then the variable:

$$t = r \cdot \sqrt{\frac{n - 2}{1 - r^2}} \tag{3.2}$$

has a Student's t-distribution under the null, zero correlation, hypothesis. This approximately holds in cases of non-normal observed values if the sample sizes are large enough. We can use the t-test that was described earlier in order to assess whether a Pearson correlation coefficient calculated over a certain sample differs from 0. The aim is to test the null hypothesis that the true correlation coefficient is equal to 0, based on the value of the sample correlation coefficient r.

3.3   NONPARAMETRIC TESTS

When the test statistic distribution under the null hypothesis is unknown, nonparametric significance testing should be applied. The nonparametric tests that are commonly used in NLP setups can be divided into two families that differ with respect to their statistical power and

Algorithm 3.6 The Sign Test

Input : $\{(x_i, y_i)\}$—pairs of data samples ($i = 1, \ldots, n$).
Output : p—the p-value.

1: **for** $i = 1$ to n **do**
2:    Calculate $z_i = y_i - x_i$ and $sign(z_i)$.
3: **end for**
4: Count the number of positive and negative zs, let w to be the number of positive zs.
5: Set the sample size to be the number of non-zero zs.
6: Calculate $p = P(W \geq w)$ where $W \sim Bin(0.5)$ #for a one-sided hypothesis.

---

computational complexity. The first family consists of tests that do not consider the actual values of the evaluation measures. The second family do consider the values of the measures: they test repeated samples from the test data, and estimates the p-value based on the test statistic values in the samples. We refer to the first family as the family of *sampling-free* tests and to the second as the family of *sampling-based* tests.

The two families of tests reflect different preferences with respect to the balance between statistical power and computational efficiency. Sampling-free tests do not consider the evaluation measure values because they cannot utilize any information about the distribution of these values in their calculation, only higher-level statistics of the results such as the number of cases in which each of the algorithms performs better than the other. Consequently, their statistical power is lower than that of sampling-based tests that do consider the evaluation measure values.

Sampling-based tests, however, compensate for the lack of distributional assumptions over the data with re-sampling—a computationally intensive procedure. Sampling-based methods are hence not the optimal candidates for very large datasets. The re-sampling process allows us to estimate the properties of the distribution of the test statistic under the null hypothesis (such as the mean, median, etc.) by measuring those properties when sampling with or without replacement from an approximate distribution, which is the empirical distribution.

We consider here four commonly used sampling-free tests: the sign test and two of its variants, and the Wilcoxon signed-rank test.

Sign test   This test tests whether matched pair samples are drawn from distributions with equal medians. The test statistic is the number of examples for which algorithm A is better than algorithm B, and the null hypothesis states that given a new pair of measurements (e.g., evaluations (a_i, b_i) of the two algorithms on a new test example), a_i and b_i are equally likely to be the larger number [Gibbons and Chakraborti, 2011]. The algorithm is described in Algorithm 3.6.

Table 3.1: Contingency table for the calculation of term significance in sentiment analysis for tweets

	# of Tweets with Term w	# of Tweets w/o the Term w
# of Positive Tweets	a	b
# of Negative Tweets	c	d

Algorithm 3.7 The McNemar Test

Input : a, b, c, d as in Table 3.1.
Output : p—the p-value.

1: Calculate the test statistic $\chi^2 = \frac{(b-c)^2}{b+c}$.
2: Calculate $p = P(X \geq \chi^2)$ where $X \sim \chi^2_{(1)}$.

The sign test has limited practical implications since it only checks if algorithm A is better than B and ignores the extent of the difference. That is, the sign test is most useful when comparisons can be expressed as $x > y$, $x = y$, or $x < y$. If, instead, the observations can be expressed as numeric quantities, or as ranks, then the Wilcoxon signed-rank test will usually have greater power. The assumptions of the sign test are: (a) the data samples are i.i.d; (b) the differences come from a continuous distribution (not necessarily normal); and (c) the values are ordered. Despite its limitations, this test was applied in a variety of NLP papers, e.g., Chan et al. [2007], Collins et al. [2005], and Rush et al. [2012].

The next test is a special case of the sign test for binary classification.

McNemar's test [McNemar, 1947]   This test is designed for paired nominal observations, i.e., binary labels. The test is applied to a 2×2 contingency table, which tabulates the outcomes of two algorithms on a sample of n examples (see example in Table 3.1). The null hypothesis for this test states that the marginal probability of each outcome (label one or label two) is the same for both algorithms. That is, when applying both algorithms on the same data we would expect them to be correct/incorrect on the same proportion of items. Under the null hypothesis, with a sufficiently large number of disagreements between the algorithms, the test statistic $\chi^2 = \frac{(b-c)^2}{b+c}$ has a distribution of χ^2 with one degree of freedom (see Algorithm 3.7). This test is appropriate for binary classification tasks, and has been indeed used in such NLP works, e.g., sentiment classification [Blitzer et al., 2006, Ziser and Reichart, 2017]. The *Cochran's Q test* [Cochran, 1950] generalizes the McNemar's test for multi-class classification setups.

The sign test and its variants consider only pairwise ranks: which algorithm performs better on each test example. In NLP setups, however, we also have access to the evaluation measure

Algorithm 3.8 The Wilcoxon Signed-rank Test

Input : $\{(x_i, y_i)\}$—pairs of data samples ($i = 1, \ldots, n$).
Output : p—the p-value.

1: **for** $i = 1$ to n **do**
2:     Calculate $z_i = |y_i - x_i|$ and let $sgn(z_i) = sign(y_i - x_i)$.
3: **end for**
4: Set the sample size N to be the number of non-zero zs.
5: Order the N pairs from smallest absolute difference to largest absolute difference.
6: Rank the pairs, starting with the pair with the smallest non-zero absolute difference as 1. Ties receive a rank equal to the average of the ranks they span. Let R_i denote the rank.
7: Calculate the test statistic $W = \sum_{i=1}^{N} sgn(z_i) \cdot R_i$, the sum of the signed ranks.
8: As N increases, the sampling distribution of W converges to a normal distribution. For $N \geq 20$, a Z-score can be calculated as $Z = \frac{W}{\sigma_W}$, where $\sigma_W = \sqrt{\frac{N(N+1)(2N+1)}{6}}$.

values, and this allows us to rank the differences between the algorithms. The Wilcoxon signed-rank test makes use of such a rank and hence, while it does not consider the evaluation measure values, it is more powerful than the sign test and its variants. In some cases, the observations for all subjects can be assigned a rank value $[1, 2, 3, \ldots)$. If the observations can be ranked, and each observation in a pair is a random sample from a symmetric distribution, then Wilcoxon signed-rank test is a better option than the sign test since it is more statistically powerful.

Wilcoxon signed-rank test [Wilcoxon, 1945]   Like the sign test variants, this test is used when comparing two matched samples, e.g., UAS values of two dependency parsers on a set of sentences. Its null hypothesis is that the differences follow a symmetric distribution around zero. The test is applied in the following way—first, the absolute values of the differences are ranked; Then, each rank gets a sign according to the sign of the difference. The Wilcoxon test statistic sums these signed ranks. The test is actually applicable for most NLP setups and it has been used widely (e.g., Søgaard [2013], Søgaard et al. [2014], Yang and Mitchell [2017]) due to its improved power compared to the sign test variants. The algorithm is depicted in Algorithm 3.8.

As noted above, sampling-free tests trade statistical power for efficiency. Sampling-based methods take the opposite approach. This family is largely divide to two: permutation/randomization tests [Noreen, 1989] and the paired bootstrap [Efron and Tibshirani, 1994]. These tests estimate the test statistic distribution and the p-value by repeatedly sampling, with or without replacement, from the test data. Next, we describe the Fisher–Pitman permutation test and the paired bootstrap test.

Algorithm 3.9 The Fisher–Pitman Permutation Test

Input : $\{(x_i, y_i)\}$—pairs of data samples $(i = 1, \ldots, n)$.
Output : p—the p-value.

1: Set $count = 0$.
2: Calculate $\bar{X} = \frac{1}{n} \sum_{i=1}^{n} x_i$ and $\bar{Y} = \frac{1}{n} \sum_{i=1}^{n} y_i$.
3: Set $T_{obs} = \bar{X} - \bar{Y}$.
4: Set $P = \{$all possible permutations of $(x_1, y_1, x_2, y_2, \ldots, x_n, y_n)\}$.
5: **for** $k = 1$ to $(2n)!$ **do**
6:    Let p_k be the kth permutation in P.
7:    Calculate $\bar{X} = \frac{1}{n} \sum_{i=1}^{n} p_{ki}$ and $\bar{Y} = \frac{1}{n} \sum_{i=n+1}^{2n} p_{ki}$.
8:    **if** $\bar{X} - \bar{Y} > T_{obs}$ **then**
9:       $count = count + 1$
10:   **end if**
11:   Calculate $p = \frac{count}{(2n)!}$ #for a one-sided hypothesis.
12: **end for**

Fisher–Pitman permutation test   This test estimates the test statistic distribution under the null hypothesis by calculating the values of this statistic under all possible labels (permutations) of the test set. The (two-sided) p-value of the test is calculated as the proportion of these permutations where the absolute difference was greater than or equal to the absolute value of the difference in the output of the algorithm.

For example, if we have the F-scores of two algorithms we applied on the same dataset in the task of NER, and we wish to determine if algorithm has a different F-score than algorithm B on dataset X, then randomly permuting (swapping) the results for algorithm A and algorithm B on any test sentence $x_i \in X$ should have no effect on F-score. In this test we examine all possible swaps between test examples and the p-value is the fraction of permutations for which the difference in F-score was greater than the original sample. The algorithm is demonstrated in Algorithm 3.9.

Obviously, permutation tests are computationally intensive due to the exponentially large number of possible permutations. In practice, *approximate randomization tests* are used where a pre-defined limited number of permutations are drawn from the space of all possible permutations, without replacements (see, e.g., Riezler and Maxwell [2005] in the context of machine translation). This method is an approximate method to the permutation test and hence has lower statistical power, but it is applicable for real world applications. The bootstrap test [Efron and Tibshirani, 1994] is based on a closely related idea. The permutation test assesses significance conditioned on the original test data, the permutations do not change the data itself. To also model the variability in the data, we can use the statistical bootstrap [Efron and Tibshirani, 1994].

Paired bootstrap test   This test is very similar to the approximate randomization version of the permutation test, with the difference that the sampling is done with replacements, i.e., an example from the original test data can appear more than once in a sample. The bootstrap procedure tests if algorithm A scores the same as algorithm B using a test dataset from the same distribution of the original test dataset X but not necessarily the original dataset X. The idea of bootstrap is to use the samples as surrogate populations, for the purpose of approximating the sampling distribution of the test statistic. The p-value is calculated in a similar manner to the permutation test.

Bootstrap was used with a variety of NLP tasks, including machine translation, text summarization, and semantic parsing (e.g., Koehn [2004], Li et al. [2017], Wu et al. [2017], and Ouchi et al. [2017]). The test is less effective for small test sets, as it assumes that the test set distribution does not deviate too much from the population distribution. On the other hand, the approximate randomization version of the permutation test does not assume the samples it approximates to be representative of the populations from which they are drawn, so it is more robust than the bootstrap test, which is in turn more prone to type I and type II errors [Cohen, 1995, Noreen, 1989].

Clearly, sampling-based methods are computationally intensive and can be intractable for very large datasets, even with modern computing power. In such cases, sampling-free methods are an available alternative.

In this chapter, we presented various parametric and nonparametric tests. We put an emphasis on the paired setup which is suitable for cases where we compare the performance of several NLP algorithms on the same dataset. We now proceed to explore statistical significance tests for NLP. In the next chapter we describe a variety of NLP tasks, applications, and evaluation measures, and provide a matching between each case and its suitable significance test.

CHAPTER 4

Statistical Significance in NLP

In previous chapters we presented the concept of statistical significance and discussed significance test families—parametric and nonparametric—as well as the properties of the actual significance tests. We now wish to continue exploring these notions in view of the NLP domain. We begin by diving into the world of NLP, presenting various tasks and their corresponding evaluation measures. We then provide a simple decision tree that helps guide the choice of which statistical test type should be chosen for the different cases. After that, we provide a table that conveniently matches the aforementioned NLP tasks and measures with their suitable statistical significance tests. Last, we shortly discuss a recent practical issue that many researchers encounter when wanting to apply the statistical significance testing framework with big testsets.

4.1 NLP TASKS AND EVALUATION MEASURES

We start with a brief description of a handful of prominent NLP tasks and applications. Our goal is by no means to provide a comprehensive survey, but rather to introduce the evaluation challenges in the field and the corresponding performance measures. One way to classify NLP tasks is by their granular input units (words, sentences, larger text chunks) and the linguistic level they address: either syntax (structure) or semantics (meaning). Next, we aim to provide a sample that covers this space of possibilities.

Language modeling is the task of assigning a probability distribution to sequences of words in a language. This allows the calculation of the likelihood of a given word (or word sequence) to follow a given sequence of words. This task is often evaluated using the perplexity (PP) measure which is a measurement of how well a probability distribution predicts a sample, or in the case of language modeling how well the model predicts the suffix of a word sequence given its prefix:

$$PP(w_1 w_2 \ldots w_N) = P(w_1 w_2 \ldots w_N)^{-\frac{1}{N}} = \sqrt[N]{\prod_{i=1}^{N} P(w_i | w_1 \ldots w_{i-1})}. \qquad (4.1)$$

The task is also evaluated using the bits-per-character (BPC) measure which is equivalent in its spirit to perplexity ($PP \approx 2^{avg*BPC}$), where avg is the average number of bits per word [Graves, 2013].

Word similarity is the task of specifying the degree of resemblance in meaning between words. The similarity relationship may vary in its definition according to the application it is required for, whether for finding synonyms to substitute words or finding hyponyms and hypernyms for sentence meaning expansion. The standard evaluation for this task is to compare the word pair similarity scores produced by the algorithm to the similarity scores given by human annotators. To compare these two sets of scores an evaluation metric of correlation is usually applied, either correlation between the actual scores as measured by the Pearson correlation coefficient:

$$r_{xy} = \frac{\sum_{i=1}^{n}(x_i - \bar{x})(y_i - \bar{y})}{\sqrt{\sum_{i=1}^{n}(x_i - \bar{x})^2}\sqrt{\sum_{i=1}^{n}(y_i - \bar{y})^2}}, \tag{4.2}$$

or correlation between word pair ranks as measured by the Spearman's correlation coefficient:

$$r_s = 1 - \frac{6\sum d_i^2}{n(n^2 - 1)}, \tag{4.3}$$

where d_i is the difference between the ranks of the ith word pair.

Sequence labeling is the task of assigning each token in a sequence a label from a fixed label set. NLP variants of sequence labeling include Part of Speech (POS) tagging, Named Entity Recognition (NER), and Syntactic Chunking, also known as shallow parsing. POS tagging is the task of assigning a part of speech to each word in a sentence, NER is about detecting (potentially multi-word) named entities like person or organization names, and chunking aims at identifying syntactic constituents within a sentence, like noun or verb phrases.

An important aspect of the evaluation is that most of the sequence items (usually words) often do not belong to one of the classes—we refer to these items as items that belong to a non-class label. The standard evaluation measure for tasks like NER and chunking is the F1 score because researchers often seek to report a balanced measure that represents the precision and recall of the detection task, and F1 is exactly the harmonic mean of these quantities. The precision, recall and F1 are calculated using the following terms:

- true positives (tp): the number of words (sequence items) that are correctly labeled with the class label;

- false positives (fp): the number of words (sequence items) that are incorrectly labeled with the class label; and

- false negatives (fn): the number of words (sequence items) that are incorrectly labeled with the non-class label or with another class label.

Then the per-class precision, recall and F1 are defined as:

$$precision = \frac{tp}{tp + fp}$$ (4.4)

$$recall = \frac{tp}{tp + fn}$$

$$F_1 = 2 \cdot \frac{precision \cdot recall}{precision + recall}.$$

The F1 score is calculated per label, and an average of all scores can be calculated in two manners: micro-F1 and macro-F1. Macro-average computes the metric independently for each label and then takes the average (hence treating all labels equally), whereas micro-average aggregates the contributions of all labels to compute the average metric. For l possible labels, the equations of micro/macro precision and recall are presented below, and the micro/macro F1 is the harmonic average of the corresponding precision and recall:

$$precision_{micro} = \frac{\sum_{i=1}^{l} tp_i}{\sum_{i=1}^{l} tp_i + fp_i}$$ (4.5)

$$recall_{micro} = \frac{\sum_{i=1}^{l} tp_i}{\sum_{i=1}^{l} tp_i + fn_i}$$

$$precision_{macro} = \frac{\sum_{i=1}^{l} precision_i}{l}$$

$$recall_{macro} = \frac{\sum_{i=1}^{l} recall_i}{l}.$$

Syntactic parsing   is the task of assigning a syntactic structure to a sentence. There are several common syntactic representations in the NLP literature. Here, we briefly describe the two most common: constituency and dependency. Constituency parse trees (Figure 4.1) are tree graphs where words are leaves with part of speech tags as parents and the other tree nodes correspond to phrases (constituents). Dependency parse trees (Figure 4.1) are tree graphs where the nodes correspond to words, and each word is a modifier of a single head word, which is represented as an arc from the head to the modifier.

The standard evaluation metric for constituency parsing is the aforementioned F1 score, computed over the constituents of the tree. In this computation each constituent is represented by the index of the first and the last word it spans, and by its syntactic category. For example, the left NP (noun phrase) constituent of the tree in Figure 4.1 will be encoded as (NP,1,2). Practically, the comparison is between two constituent sets—the one of the algorithm's tree and the one of a human generated tree.

For dependency parsing the standard evaluation metrics are UAS and LAS which measure the number of correct edges, either unlabeled (UAS) or labeled (LAS) and is equivalent to measuring the accuracy of edge assignments to the words of the input sentence.

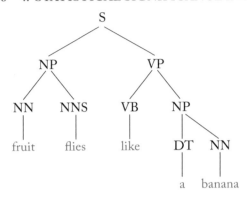

(a) An example constituency parse tree   (b) An example unlabeled dependency parse tree

Figure 4.1: Examples of parse trees.

Semantic parsing   is the task of mapping a natural language utterance into a formal meaning representation on which a machine can operate. Various types of such semantic representations can be found in the literature and they are mostly based on logical forms. Representations may be an executable language such as SQL or more abstract representations such as Abstract Meaning Representation (AMR) [Banarescu et al., 2013]. The standard evaluation metric for this task involves 0/1 accuracy scores, either between the gold and learned trees, or between relevant pieces of information extracted from these trees, e.g., answers to a given question. An example of natural language utterances with logical forms in lambda-DCS and lambda calculus [Liang, 2013] is as follows:

- Utterance: "people who have lived in Seattle"

- Lambda calculus: $\lambda x.\exists e.\textbf{PlacesLived}(x, e) \land \textbf{Location}(e, \textbf{Seattle})$

- Lambda DCS: **PlacesLived.Location.Seattle**

Coreference resolution   is the task of finding all expressions that refer to the same entity in a text. It is an important task that helps improving the performance of many higher-level NLP tasks mostly because it helps to solve ambiguities [Peng et al., 2015]. The standard evaluation measure for this task is the F1 score.

Sentiment classification   is the task of classifying the sentiment polarity of a given text—usually a sentence or a document. Simply put, given a text, the task is to detect whether the sentiment expressed in it is positive or negative, but the prediction task can also be of the sentiment polarity (e.g., on a 1–5 scale). The standard evaluation metric for the binary version of this task is accuracy, but its polarity variant is usually evaluated with a root mean square error

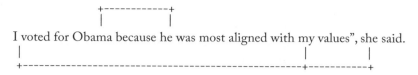

Figure 4.2: Coreference resolution example.

(RMSE) metric (Equation 4.6):

$$RMSE = \sqrt{\frac{\sum_{i=1}^{N}(y_i - \hat{y}_i)^2}{N}}. \tag{4.6}$$

Machine translation (MT)   is the task in which an algorithm should translate a text from one language to another. Evaluation in this task is more challenging than in the previously mentioned tasks because a text in one language may have multiple correct translations in another language and the translation quality often has a subjective aspect.

There are several standard automatic evaluation metrics for machine translation, and more evaluation metrics are constantly proposed. Some known metrics are: BLUE [Papineni et al., 2002] (formula below), METEOR [Banerjee and Lavie, 2005], and word error rate (WER). For example, BLEU is calculated by averaging over the n-gram matches for every hypothesis sentence S in the test corpus C and multiplying by a brevity penalty BP:

$$p_n = \frac{\sum_{S \in C} \sum_{ngram \in S} COUNT_{match}(ngram)}{\sum_{S \in C} \sum_{ngram \in S} COUNT(ngram)} \tag{4.7}$$

$$BP = \begin{cases} e^{1-len(candidate)/len(corpus-ref)} & \text{if } len(candidate) \geq len(corpus-ref); \\ 1 & \text{otherwise.} \end{cases}$$

$$BLEU = BP \cdot \exp\left(\frac{1}{N}\sum_{n=1}^{N} \log p_n\right).$$

It is common to evaluate the automatic evaluation metrics based on their correlation with human judgments, but, unfortunately, this correlation is far from perfect. Yet, automatic evaluation metrics still play a key role in MT evaluation.

Question answering   is a task explored both within NLP and Information Retrieval (IR). This task focuses on designing systems that automatically answer textual questions presented by humans. Since this task is researched both within NLP and IR, the evaluation metrics are often the ones used in IR, mostly precision@k and recall@k. Precision at k is the proportion of recommended items in the top-k set that are relevant and recall at k is the proportion of relevant items found in the top-k recommendations.

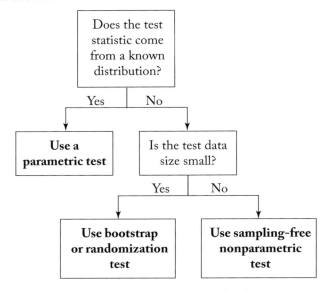

Figure 4.3: Decision tree for statistical significance test selection.

As noted above, our goal in the above brief survey has been to briefly present a handful of prominent NLP tasks and discuss their evaluation measures. Below we provide a simple decision tree that guides the reader to choose an appropriate significance test for NLP tasks.

4.2   DECISION TREE FOR SIGNIFICANCE TEST SELECTION

Now that we have acquainted ourselves with a few prominent NLP tasks and their corresponding evaluation metrics, we continue in our goal toward finding a suitable statistical significance test for each specific case. Before we continue on to the next section, in which we present a matching between evaluation metrics and significance tests, we wish to begin by portraying a simple decision mechanism to help researchers choose the test family that is appropriate for their setup. The decision tree in Figure 4.3 provides an illustration of our proposed process.

The fundamental question we should ask ourselves is if the distribution of the test statistic under the null hypothesis is known. If that is the case, then parametric tests are most appropriate. These tests are more statistically powerful and less computationally intensive compared to their nonparametric counterparts. The stronger statistical power of parametric tests stems from the stronger, parametric assumptions they make, while the higher computational demand of some nonparametric tests is the result of their sampling process. This is because in addition to checking the significance of results, the nonparametric tests approximate or estimate other parameters that are unknown, which lowers the statistical power of the test.

When the distribution of the test statistic is unknown, we should consider using one of several types of nonparametric tests. The first nonparametric family of choice is that of sampling-based tests. These tests consider the actual values of the evaluation metrics and are not restricted to higher-order properties (e.g., ranks) of the observed values—their statistical power is hence higher. As noted in Riezler and Maxwell [2005], in the case where the distributional assumptions of the parametric tests are violated, sampling-based tests have more statistical power than parametric tests.

Nonetheless, as we previously discussed, sampling-based tests are computationally intensive—the exact permutation test, for example, requires the generation of all 2^n data permutations, where n is the number of points in the dataset. To overcome this, approximate randomization can be used, as was done, e.g., by Yeh [2000] for test sets of more than 20 points. The other alternative for very large datasets are sampling-free tests that are less powerful but are computationally feasible.

Following this decision process, we are now equipped with tools for making the decision of what type of test to choose—be it parametric or nonparametric, and if the latter is appropriate then what type of nonparametric test would be most effective. To take our recommendations to a more granular level, we next provide a specific mapping between evaluation measures and significance tests.

4.3   MATCHING BETWEEN EVALUATION MEASURES AND STATISTICAL SIGNIFICANCE TESTS

In this book, we aim to make the comparison between NLP algorithms in a statistically sound manner a process that is as comfortable as possible for researchers. For this purpose, it is only natural to describe a variety of the most prominent NLP tasks alongside their respective evaluation measures (see previous section), and provide a manual of sorts, matching between tasks, evaluation measures, and the appropriate statistical significance test.

Table 4.1 provides, for the prominent evaluation measures in NLP, a valid statistical test as well as the assumptions made upon using each test. For each measure we provide both parametric and nonparametric alternatives that can be used under certain assumptions.

The parametric tests discussed here assume that the data is normally distributed. This assumption is likely to hold when using evaluation measures that calculate an average of counts of correct classifications. When the normality assumption that accompanies these tests holds in practice, they have higher statistical power than their nonparametric counterparts proposed in the table, hence it is recommended to use them. Otherwise, one should use nonparametric tests that do not make any such assumptions. We marked in the parametric test column cases where it is unlikely to assume normality by — .

For example, in the case of recall, precision, and F-score, [Yeh, 2000] described why the t-test can only be used for the former. For other evaluation measures, one can test if the data is normally distributed by applying statistical tests that check for normality (e.g., Shapiro–Wilk,

Table 4.1: Statiscal test (*Continues*)

Evaluation Measure	Description	Parametric Test	Nonparametric Test	Exemplary Task	Assumptions Comments
Contingency table/ confusion matrix	2×2 table[1] which presents the outcomes of an algorithm on a sample of n data points: $\begin{array}{c\|c} \text{\# tp} & \text{\# fp} \\ \hline \text{\# fn} & \text{\# tn} \end{array}$	—	McNemar's test	Binary sentiment classification	tp (true positive), fp (false positive), fn (false negative), tn (true negative)
Exact match	Percentage of predictions that match any one of the ground truth answers exactly	t-test	Bootstrap/ permutation	Question answering	1, 2
Accuracy	Proportion of true results (both true positives and true negatives) among the total number of cases examined[2]	t-test	Bootstrap/ permutation	Sequence labeling	1, 2
Recall	$\dfrac{\text{true positive}}{\text{true positive+false negative}}$ [3]	t-test	Bootstrap/ permutation	Phrase-based (constituent) parsing	1, 2, 6
Precision	$\dfrac{\text{true positive}}{\text{true positive+false negative}}$ [3]	—	Bootstrap/ permutation	Phrase-based (constituent) parsing	2, 6
F score	$F_\beta = (1 + \beta^2) \cdot \dfrac{\text{precision} \cdot \text{recall}}{(\beta^2 \cdot \text{precision}) + \text{recall}}$	—	Bootstrap/ permutation	Semantic parsing	2, 6
Perplexity	Measurement of how well a probability distribution or probability model predicts a sample[4]	—	Wilcoxon signed-rank test	Language modeling	5
Spearman correlation	Measure of rank correlation between the ranking produced by two algorithms[5]	Z-test	Bootstrap/ permutation	Word similarity	2,3
Pearson correlation	Measure of the linear correlation between the results of two algorithms[6]	Z-test	Bootstrap/ permutation	Word similarity	2,3

Table 4.1: (*Continued*) Statiscal test

UAS (sentence-level)	Unlabeled attachment score [Kübler et al., 2009]	t-test	Bootstrap/ permutation	Dependency parsing	1,2,4
LAS (sentence-level)	Labeled attachment score [Kübler et al., 2009]	t-test	Bootstrap/ permutation	Dependency parsing	1,2,4
ROUGE	[Lin, 2004]	—	Bootstrap/ permutation	Summariza-tion	2
BLEU	[Papineni et al., 2002]	—	Bootstrap/ permutation	Machine translation	2
METEOR	[Banerjee and Lavie, 2005]	—	Bootstrap/ permutation	Machine translation	2
PINC	[Chen et al., 2011]	—	Bootstrap/ permutation	Paraphrasing	2
CIDEr	[Vedantam et al., 2015]	—	Bootstrap/ permutation	Image description generation	2
MUC, B^3, $CEAF_e$, BLANC	[Bagga and Baldwin, 1998, Lee et al., 2012, Luo, 2005, Vilain et al., 1995]	—	Bootstrap/ permutation	Coreference resolution	2, 7
Krippen-dorf's alpha, Cohen's kappa	Statistical measures of agreement [Cohen, 1960, Krippendorff, 2011]	—	Bootstrap/ permutation	Annotation reliability	2
MRR	Mean reciprocal rank, used for algorithms that produce a list of possible responses to a sample of queries, ordered by probability of correctness[7]	—	Bootstrap/ permutation	Question answering, information retrieval	2

[1] https://en.wikipedia.org/wiki/Confusion_matrix
[2] https://en.wikipedia.org/wiki/Accuracy_and_precision
[3] https://en.wikipedia.org/wiki/Precision_and_recall
[4] https://en.wikipedia.org/wiki/Perplexity
[5] https://en.wikipedia.org/wiki/Spearman%27s_rank_correlation_coefficient
[6] https://en.wikipedia.org/wiki/Pearson_correlation_coefficient
[7] https://en.wikipedia.org/wiki/Mean_reciprocal_rank

Kolmogorov–Smirnov, or Anderson–Darling as described in Chapter 3). In this table, we only mention a parametric test when we consider it likely to assume normality.

An additional important distinction has to do with paired vs. non-paired tests. When comparing the performance of two algorithms that are applied to the same dataset, the paired version of the statistical significance test should be preferred, e.g., the matched-pair t-test. Using tests that assume independent samples in such a setup will results in conclusions that are not statistically sound. An implementation of paired versions of all statistical tests presented here as well as of other tests can be found at https://github.com/rtmdrr/testSignificanceNLP.

ASSUMPTIONS AND COMMENTS

1. t-test: assuming that an average count of correct classifications is normally distributed.

2. Bootstrap: assuming the dataset is representative of the entire population.

3. Fisher transformation: $F(r) = \frac{1}{2} \ln \frac{1+r}{1-r}$.

   - For Spearman: $\sqrt{\frac{n-3}{1.06}} F(r)$ approximately follows a standard normal distribution.
   - For Pearson: the Fisher transformation approximately follows a normal distribution with a mean of $F(\rho)$ and a standard deviation of $\frac{1}{\sqrt{n-3}}$, where n is the sample size. One can use this to apply the Z-test for significance test.

4. UAS and LAS are actually accuracy measures since attachment scores depend on error counts and not false positives and negatives.

5. Wilcoxon signed-rank test: since the label space of a language can be very large (it is equal to the vocabulary size), non-sampling nonparametric tests are preferable.

6. See Yeh [2000] for explanations.

7. All measures used for evaluating coreference resolution are functions of precision and recall. Since parametric tests are not suitable in the case of precision, these tests are also not valid for these measures.

4.4   SIGNIFICANCE WITH LARGE TEST SAMPLES

In addition to the question on the distribution of the test statistic, there is another prominent practical issue when it comes to NLP research. It is well recognized that when using large test-sets it becomes "too easy" to reject the null hypothesis that claims there is no effect, or in our case, significant difference in the performance of the two compared algorithms. In other words, when working with large test-sets, small effects are often significant even when setting the significance level to be very low. In the current era of large datasets, the validity and relevance of statistical significance testing may hence be questioned.

Algorithm 4.10 The Paired Sample t-test with δ effect size

Input : Paired samples, δ—effect size.
Output : p—the p-value.
Notations : D differences between two paired samples, d_i the ith observation in D, n the sample size, $\bar{d}$ the sample mean of the differences, $\hat{\sigma}$ the sample standard deviation of the differences, T the critical value of a t-distribution with $n - 1$ degrees of freedom, t the t-statistic (t-test statistic) for a paired sample t-test.

1: Calculate the sample mean—$\bar{d} = \frac{1}{n} \sum_{i=1}^{n} d_i$.
2: Calculate the sample standard deviation - $\hat{\sigma} = \sqrt{\frac{1}{n-1} \left(\sum_{i=1}^{n} d_i^2 - (\sum_{i=1}^{n} d_i)^2 \right)}$.
3: Calculate the test statistic—$t = \frac{\bar{d} - \delta}{\hat{\sigma} / \sqrt{n}}$.
4: Find the p-value in the t-distribution table, using the predefined significance level and $n - 1$ degrees of freedom.

First let us explain why the probability of rejecting the null hypothesis is high when working with large datasets. Considering all statistical tests and all p-value calculations presented above, the size of the test-set, n, affects every one of them. This is because when estimating the probability of having a type I error, one has to estimate the standard deviation of the data, which is generally very small for large datasets. The outcome is a very small p-value, which leads to the rejection of the null hypothesis in most cases.

In general, if an effect size (i.e., the difference in performance between the two algorithms) is large, it will be noticeable and hence statistically significant in both small and large datasets. If an effect size is too small to confirm with a small dataset, it is possible to increase the sample size, reduce the variance and get the desired effect: A practice that is known as "p-hacking". Nonetheless, the results of the model comparison may have no practical significance, may be unrepeatable in small scale settings, or may be invalid due to the persistence of biases that were not eliminated when the sample size was increased.

This problem is the subject of an active discussion (for example, see Hofmann [2015]). While alternatives to the hypothesis testing framework have been proposed in the context of this discussion, in this book we consider a simple and effective solution within this framework. Namely, instead of testing the hypothesis that there is some difference between the performance of the algorithms, i.e., testing if $\delta(X) > 0$ as in Equation (2.4), in the case where we have a large test-set we should hypothesize about a more substantial effect size, i.e., testing if $\delta(X) > \delta$, where $\delta > 0$. The changes that should be made to the significance test for this type of hypothesis are minor, see for example Algorithm 4.10 for the modified t-test.

CHAPTER 5

Deep Significance

In the past, most supervised NLP models have been linear (or log-linear), convex, and relatively simple, e.g., Finkel et al. [2008], Toutanova et al. [2003], and Ritter et al. [2011]. Hence, their training was often deterministic and the number of configurations a model could have was rather small—decisions about model design were usually limited to feature selection and the selection of one of a few loss functions. Consequently, when one model performed better than another on unseen data it was safe to argue that the winning model was generally better, especially when the results were statistically significant.[1]

With the recent emergence of Deep Neural Networks (DNNs), data-driven performance comparison has become much more complicated. While models such as LSTM [Hochreiter and Schmidhuber, 1997], BiLSTM [Schuster and Paliwal, 1997], and the transformer [Vaswani et al., 2017] improve the state of the art in many NLP tasks (e.g., Dozat and Manning [2017], Hershcovich et al. [2017], Yadav and Bethard [2018]), it is much more difficult to compare the performance of algorithms that are based on these models. This is because the loss functions of these models are non-convex [Dauphin et al., 2014], making the solution to which they converge (a local minimum or a saddle point) sensitive to random weight initialization and the order of training examples. Moreover, as these complex models are not fully understood, their training is often enhanced by heuristics such as random dropouts [Srivastava et al., 2014] that introduces another level of non-determinism to the training process. Finally, the increased model complexity results in a much larger number of configurations, governed by a large space of hyper-parameters for model properties such as the number of layers and the number of neurons in each layer.

With so many degrees of freedom governed by random and arbitrary values, when comparing two DNNs it is not possible to consider a single test-set evaluation score for each model. If we do that, we might compare just the best models that someone happened to train rather than the methods themselves. Instead, it is necessary to compare between the score distributions generated by different runs of each of the models.

This chapter is divided in five. We first discuss the sources of non-determinism in DNNs. Then we propose a framework for statistically significant comparison between non-deterministic models and particularly DNNs. Then, based on the proposed framework, we analyze existing

---

[1]Note that this discussion of linear models is a bit over-simplified. Linear model training has never been fully deterministic in practice, even for models with only a handful of features like minimum error rate training in machine translation. One of the methods for coping with uncertainty that we discuss below, was in fact designed for dealing with the non-determinism of linear models [Clark et al., 2011].

methods for comparison between DNNs and demonstrate that they fail to respect at least some of the three criteria in our proposed framework. We next present our proposed evaluation and demonstrate that it does respect our proposed framework. We conclude with extensive empirical analysis where we compare our proposed evaluation with previous practices. This chapter is based on our ACL 2019 paper [Dror et al., 2019].

5.1 PERFORMANCE VARIANCE IN DEEP NEURAL NETWORK MODELS

In this section we discuss the source of non-determinism in DNNs, focusing on hyper-parameter configurations and random choices.

Hyper-parameter Configurations DNNs are complex models governed by a variety of hyper-parameters. A formal definition of a hyper-parameter, differentiating it from a standard parameter, is usually a parameter whose value is set before the learning process begins. We can roughly say that hyper-parameters determine the structure of the model and particular algorithmic decisions related, e.g., to its optimization. Some popular structure-related hyper-parameters in the DNN literature are the number of layers, layer sizes, activation functions, loss functions, window sizes, stride values, and parameter initialization methods. Some optimization-(training) related hyper-parameters are the optimization algorithms, learning rates, number of epochs, momentum, and mini-batch sizes, whether or not to use optimization heuristics such as gradient clipping and gradient normalization, and sampling and ordering methods of the training data.

To decide on the hyper-parameter values, it is standard to explore several configurations and observe which performs best on an unseen, held-out dataset, commonly referred to as the development set. For some hyper-parameters (e.g., the learning rate and the optimization algorithm) the range of feasible values reflects the intuitions of the model author, and the tuned value provides some insight about the model and the data. However, for many other hyper-parameters (e.g., the number of neurons in each layer of the model and the number of epochs of the optimization algorithm) the range of values and the selected values are quite arbitrary. Hence, although hyper-parameters can be tuned on development data, the distribution of model's evaluation scores across these configurations is of interest, especially when considering the hyper-parameters with the more arbitrary values.

Random Choices There are also hyper-parameters that do not follow the above tuning logic. These include some of the hyper-parameters that govern the random ordering of the training examples, the dropout process and the initialization of the model parameters. The values of these hyper-parameters are often set randomly.

In other cases, randomization is introduced to the model without an explicit hyper-parameter. For example, a popular initialization method for DNN weights is the Xavier method [Glorot and Bengio, 2010]. In this method, the initial weights are sampled from a

Gaussian distribution with a mean of 0 and a standard deviation of $\sqrt{2/n_i}$, where n_i is the number of input units of the ith layer.

Being non-convex, the convergent point of DNNs is deeply affected by these random effects. Unfortunately, exploring all possible random seeds is impossible both because they form an uncountable set and because their values are uninterpretable and it is even hard to decide on the relevant search space for their values. This dictates the need for reporting model results with multiple random choices.

5.2   A DEEP NEURAL NETWORK COMPARISON FRAMEWORK

To ensure a simple and effective comparison between two DNN models, we propose three criteria that a high-quality DNN comparison tool should meet. We assume here that due to the inherent non-determinism of DNNs, comparing between such models requires an access to a set of performance scores generated by each model. This set of scores can be generated by running the model with different values of its random parameters or with different hyper-parameter configurations. Here we do not discuss the way the score set is generated, but leave it to the practitioner to decide which parameters and hyper-parameters are not inherent to the model architecture and cannot be assumed to have a fixed value when reporting the model performance.

Our proposal stems from the framework of statistically significant hypothesis testing that was discussed in Chapter 2, and we believe that it provides a natural extension to the non-deterministic case. The criteria are as follows.

(a) Since we observe only a sample from the population score distribution of each model, the decision should be **significant** under well justified statistical assumptions. Performing a valid statistical test assures that future runs of the superior model are likely to get higher scores than future runs of the inferior model because the type I error is bounded by a predefined constant.

(b) The decision mechanism should be **powerful**, being able to make decisions in most possible decision tasks. For example, in the case of statistical hypothesis testing the statistical power of the test should be high.

(c) Since both models depend on random decisions, it is likely that none of them is promised to be superior over the other in all cases, e.g., with all possible random seeds. A powerful comparison tool should hence augment its decision with a **confidence score**, reflecting the probability that the superior model will indeed produce a better output.

We next survey the current practices of DNN comparison and check whether or not they respect the above three criteria.

5.3   EXISTING METHODS FOR DEEP NEURAL NETWORK COMPARISON

Given two algorithms, each associated with a set of test-set evaluation scores, the goal of an evaluation method is to determine which algorithm, if any, is superior. The test-set evaluation scores are generated when running two different DNNs with various hyper-parameter configurations or random seeds. For both DNNs, the performance is measured using the same evaluation measure over the same dataset, without loss of generality we assume that higher values of the measure are better. To be as general as possible, the number of scores may vary between the DNNs.

Several methods have been proposed for the comparison between the score distributions of two DNNs. We now discuss these methods.

Collection of Statistics (COS)   This approach is based on the analysis of statistics of the empirical score distributions. For example, Reimers and Gurevych [2018] averaged the test-set scores and applied the Welch t-test [Welch, 1947] for comparing between the means. Notice that Welch's t-test is based on the assumption that the test-set scores are drawn from a normal distribution—an assumption that has not been validated for DNN score distributions. Hence, this method does not meet criterion (a) that requires the comparison method to check for statistical significance under realistic assumptions. Moreover, comparing only the mean of two distributions is not always sufficient for making predictions about future comparisons between the algorithms.

Other statistics such as the standard deviation, median, and the minimum and maximum values are often also relevant. For example, it might be that the mean of algorithm A is indeed larger than that of algorithm B, but A's standard deviation is also much larger, making prediction very challenging. In cases where the different statistics indicate different conclusions this method is indecisive, i.e., violating criterion (b) which requires the comparison test to be powerful.

Another example is Clark et al. [2011] where the authors estimated the variability of multiple optimizer replications in the task of machine translation. For this aim they estimated statistics such as the standard deviation on the training, development, and test datasets. Based on this idea they compared two MT systems using the approximate randomization test, which took into account all the optimizer replications of each MT system. Note, however, that this method only accounts for the variability resulted from optimizer instability, which, while important, is surely not the only source of variability, especially in complex models such as DNNs. Note also that the statistical test proposed in that work is nonparametric, and its statistical power hence depends on performing a sufficient number of repetitions.

Stochastic Order (SO)   Another approach, proposed by Reimers and Gurevych [2018], tests whether a score drawn from the distribution of algorithm A (denoted as X_A) is likely, with a probability higher than 0.5, to be larger than a score drawn from the distribution of algorithm

B (X_B). Put it formally, algorithm A is declared superior to algorithm B if:

$$P\ (X_A \geq X_B) > 0.5. \tag{5.1}$$

To test if this requirement holds based on the empirical score distributions of the two algorithms, the authors applied the Mann–Whitney U-test for independent pairs [Mann and Whitney, 1947] which tests whether there exists a stochastic order (SO) between two random variables (the test is detailed at the end of this section in Algorithm 5.11). This test is nonparametric, making no assumptions about the participating distributions except for being continuous.

We next describe the concept of SO in more details. First we define the cumulative distribution function (CDF) and the empirical CDF of a probability distribution.

For a random variable X, the CDF is defined as follows:

$$F(t) = P\ (X \leq t). \tag{5.2}$$

For a sample $\{x_1, \ldots, x_n\}$, the empirical CDF is defined as follows:

$$F_n(t) = \frac{1}{n} \sum_{i=1}^{n} 1_{x_i \leq t} = \frac{\text{number of } x_i \text{s} \leq t}{n}, \tag{5.3}$$

where $1_{x_i \leq t}$ is an indicator function that takes the value of 1 if $x_i \leq t$, and 0 otherwise.

Lehmann [1955] defines a random variable X to be *stochastically larger* than a random variable Y (denoted by $X \succeq Y$) if $F(a) \leq G(a)$ for all a (with a strict inequality for some value of a), where F and G are the CDFs of X and Y, respectively. That is, if we observe a random value sampled from the first distribution, it is likely to be larger than a random value sampled from the second distribution, and we can claim that there is SO between the two distributions.

Now we prove that if a random variable X is stochastically larger than a random variable Y, then it also holds that $P(X \geq Y) > 0.5$.

Lemma 5.1   *If $X \succeq Y$ then $P(X \geq Y) > 0.5$.*

Proof. For every two continuous random variables X, Y it holds that: $P(X \geq Y) + P(Y > X) = 1$. Let us first assume that X and Y are i.i.d and continuous. If this is the case then:

$$P(X \geq Y) + P(Y > X) = 1$$
$$P(X \geq Y) + P(X > Y) = 1$$
$$2P(X \geq Y) = 1$$
$$P(X \geq Y) = 0.5.$$

The first pass is true because X and Y are identically distributed and the second pass is true because X and Y are continuous random variables.

Assuming that the density functions of the random variables X and Y exist (which is true because they are continues variables), we can write $P(X \geq Y)$ in the following manner:

$$P(X \geq Y) = \int_{y=-\infty}^{\infty} \int_{x=y}^{\infty} f_X(x) \cdot f_Y(y) dx dy$$

$$= \int_{y=-\infty}^{\infty} f_Y(y) \cdot P(X \geq y) dy$$

$$= \int_{y=-\infty}^{\infty} f_Y(y) \cdot P(Y \geq y) dy = 0.5,$$

where the equality to 0.5 was proved above.

In our case, $X \succeq Y$. This means that X and Y are independent but are not identically distributed. By definition of SO this also means that $P(X \geq a) > P(Y \geq a)$, for all a with strict inequality for at least one value of a. We get that:

$$P(X \geq Y) = \int_{y=-\infty}^{\infty} \int_{x=y}^{\infty} f_X(x) \cdot f_Y(y) dx dy$$

$$= \int_{y=-\infty}^{\infty} f_Y(y) \cdot P(X \geq y) dy$$

$$> \int_{y=-\infty}^{\infty} f_Y(y) \cdot P(Y \geq y) dy = 0.5,$$

where the last pass holds because X is stochastically larger than Y. We get that $P(X \geq Y) > 0.5$.

$\square$

Note that the opposite direction does not always hold, i.e., it is easy to come up with an example where $P(X \geq Y) > 0.5$ but there is no SO between the two random variables. However, the opposite direction is true with an additional assumption that the CDFs do not cross one another, i.e., there are no intersection points between the two CDFs (which we do not prove here).

This lemma explains why Reimers and Gurevych [2018] employed the Mann–Whitney U-test that tests for stochastic order, while their requirement for stating that one algorithm is better than the other was that $P(X \geq Y) > 0.5$, where X is the score distribution of the superior algorithm and Y is the score distribution of the inferior algorithm.

The Mann–Whitney U-test   This test, that Reimers and Gurevych [2018] employed to test for stochastic order, is a nonparametric test with a null hypothesis that it is equally likely that a randomly selected value from one sample will be lower than or greater than a randomly selected value from a second sample, i.e., that there is no SO between the two random variables. The procedure for carrying out the test appears in Algorithm 5.11.

Algorithm 5.11 The Mann–Whitney U-test

Input : Observations from the two distributions.
Output : p—the p-value.

1: Arrange all the observations from the two distributions in order of magnitude.
2: Under each observation i, write down x_i or y_i to indicate which sample they are from.
3: Under each x_i write down the number of y_js to its left (i.e., smaller); this indicates $x_i > y_j$. Under each y_j write down the number of x_is to its left (smaller); this indicates $y_j > x_i$.
4: Add up the total number of times $x_i > y_j$ and denote the outcome by U_x. Add up the total number of times $y_j > x_i$ and denote the outcome by U_y.
5: Calculate $U = min(U_x, U_y)$ and use the statistical tables for the Mann–Whitney U-test to find the probability of observing a value of U or lower. If the test is one-sided, this is the p-value; if the test is two-sided, double this probability to obtain the p-value.

If it can be concluded from the empirical score distributions of two DNNs that SO exists between their respective population distributions, this means that one algorithm is more likely to produce higher-quality solutions than the other, and this algorithm can be declared superior. As discussed above, Reimers and Gurevych [2018] applied the Mann–Whitney U-test to test for this relationship. The U-test has high statistical power when the tested distributions are moderate-tailed, e.g., the normal distribution or the logistic distribution. For heavy tailed distribution, e.g., the Cauchy distribution, there are several alternative statistical tests that have higher statistical power, for example likelihood based tests [El Barmi and McKeague, 2013, Lee and Wolfe, 1976].

The main limitation of this approach is that SO can rarely be proven to hold based on two empirical distributions. Hence, while this approach meets our criterion (a) (testing for significance under realistic assumptions), it does not meet criterion, (b) (being a powerful test), and criterion (c) (providing a confidence score).

We will next describe another approach that does meet our three criteria. This will be our proposed approach for comparing between non-deterministic models like DNNs.

5.4   ALMOST STOCHASTIC DOMINANCE

Our starting point is that the requirement of SO is unrealistic because it means that the inequality $F(a) \leq G(a)$ should hold for every value of a. It is likely that this criterion would fail to determine dominance between two distributions even when a "reasonable" decision maker would clearly prefer one DNN over the other. We hence propose to employ a relaxed version of this criterion. We next discuss different definitions of such relaxation.

A Potential Relaxation   For $\epsilon > 0$ and random variables X and Y with CDFs F and G, respectively, we can define the following notion of ϵ-stochastic dominance: $X \succeq_\epsilon Y$ if $F(a) \leq G(a) + \epsilon$ for all a. That is, we allow the distributions to violate the SO, and hence one CDF does not have to be strictly below the other for all a.

The practical shortcomings of this definition are apparent in cases where $F(a)$ is greater than $G(a)$ for all a, with a gap bounded by, for example, $\epsilon/2$. In such cases we would not want to determine that $X \sim F$ is ϵ stochastically dominant over $Y \sim G$ because its CDF is strictly above the CDF of Y, and hence Y is stochastically larger than X. However, according to this relaxation, $X \sim F$ is indeed ϵ stochastically larger than $Y \sim G$.

Almost Stochastic Dominance   To overcome the limitations of the above straightforward approach, and define a relaxation of stochastic order, we turn to a definition that is based on the proportion of points in the domain of the participating distributions for which SO holds. That is, the test we will introduce below is based on the following two violation sets:

$$V_X = \{a : F(a) > G(a)\},$$

$$V_Y = \{a : F(a) < G(a)\}.$$

Intuitively, the variable with the smaller violation set should be declared superior and the ratio between these sets should define the gap between the distributions.

To implement this idea, del Barrio et al. [2018] defined the concept of *almost stochastic dominance*. Here we describe their work, that aims to compare two distributions, and discuss its applicability to our problem of comparing two DNN models based on the three criteria defined at the beginning of this chapter.

We start with a definition: for a CDF F, the *quantile function* associated with F is defined as:

$$F^{-1}(t) = \inf\{x : t \leq F(x)\}, t \in (0, 1). \tag{5.4}$$

It is possible to define SO using the quantile function in the following manner:

$$X \succeq Y \iff F^{-1}(t) \geq G^{-1}(t), \forall t \in (0, 1). \tag{5.5}$$

The advantage of this definition is that the domain of the quantile function is bounded between 0 and 1. This is in contrast to the CDF whose domain is unbounded.

From this definition, it is clear that a violation of the SO between X and Y occurs when $F^{-1}(t) < G^{-1}(t)$. Hence, it is easy to redefine V_X and V_Y based on the quantile functions:

$$A_X = \left\{t \in (0, 1) : F^{-1}(t) < G^{-1}(t)\right\},$$

$$A_Y = \left\{t \in (0, 1) : F^{-1}(t) > G^{-1}(t)\right\}.$$

These definitions were employed by del Barrio et al. [2018] in order to define the distance of each random variable from stochastic dominance over the other:

$$\varepsilon_{\mathcal{W}_2}(F,G) := \frac{\int_{A_X} (F^{-1}(t) - G^{-1}(t))^2 dt}{\left(W_2(F,G)\right)^2},\tag{5.6}$$

where $W_2(F,G)$, also known as the univariate L_2–Wasserstein distance between distributions, is defined as:

$$W_2(F,G) = \sqrt{\int_0^1 (F^{-1}(t) - G^{-1}(t))^2 dt}.\tag{5.7}$$

This ratio explicitly measures the distance of X (with CDF F) from stochastic dominance over Y (with CDF G) since it reflects the probability mass for which Y dominates X. The corresponding definition for the distance of Y from being stochastically dominant over X can be received from the above equations by replacing the roles of F and G and integrating over A_Y instead over A_X.

This index satisfies $0 \le \varepsilon_{\mathcal{W}_2}(F,G) \le 1$ where 0 corresponds to perfect stochastic dominance of X over Y and 1 corresponds to perfect stochastic dominance of Y over X. It also holds that $\varepsilon_{\mathcal{W}_2}(F,G) = 1 - \varepsilon_{\mathcal{W}_2}(G,F)$, and smaller values of the smaller index (which is by definition bounded between 0 and 0.5) indicate a smaller distance from stochastic dominance.

Statistical Significance Testing for ASO   Using this index it is possible to formulate the following hypothesis testing problem to test for almost stochastic dominance:

$$H_0 : \varepsilon_{\mathcal{W}_2}(F,G) \ge \epsilon\tag{5.8}$$
$$H_1 : \varepsilon_{\mathcal{W}_2}(F,G) < \epsilon$$

which tests, for a predefined $\epsilon > 0$, if the violation index is smaller than ϵ. Rejecting the null hypothesis means that the first score distribution F is almost stochastically larger than G with ϵ distance from SO.

del Barrio et al. [2018] proved that without further assumptions, H_0 will be rejected with a significance level of α if:

$$\sqrt{\frac{nm}{n+m}} \left(\varepsilon_{W_2}(F_n,G_m) - \epsilon\right) < \hat{\sigma}_{n,m} \Phi^{-1}(\alpha),\tag{5.9}$$

where F_n, G_m are the empirical CDFs with n and m samples, respectively, ϵ is the violation level, Φ^{-1} is the inverse CDF of a normal distribution and $\hat{\sigma}_{n,m}$ is the estimated variance of the value:

$$\sqrt{\frac{nm}{n+m}} \left(\varepsilon_{\mathcal{W}_2}\left(F_n^*,G_m^*\right) - \varepsilon_{\mathcal{W}_2}(F_n,G_m)\right),\tag{5.10}$$

where $\varepsilon_{\mathcal{W}_2}(F_n^*,G_m^*)$ is computed using samples X_n^*, Y_m^* from the empirical distributions F_n and G_m.[2]

---

[2]The more samples, the better. In our implementation we employ the inverse transform sampling method to generate samples.

Algorithm 5.12 Test for Almost Stochastic Dominance

Input : $\{x_1, \ldots, x_n\}$ scores from algorithm A, $\{y_1, \ldots, y_m\}$ scores from algorithm B, α— significance level.
Output : Decision which algorithm is better.

1: Build the empirical CDFs F and G based on $\{x_1, \ldots, x_n\}$ and $\{y_1, \ldots, y_m\}$, respectively.
2: Calculate the quantile functions F^{-1} and G^{-1}.
3: Calculate $\varepsilon_{W_2}(F, G) = \frac{\int_{A_X} (F^{-1}(t) - G^{-1}(t))^2 dt}{\left(W_2(F,G)\right)^2}$.
4: Estimate $\hat{\sigma}$, the standard deviation of $\varepsilon_{W_2}(F, G)$.
5: Calculate $\epsilon^{min}(F_n, G_m, \alpha)$.
6: **if** $\epsilon^{min} < 0.5$ **then**
7:   A is better than B with confidence level ϵ^{min} and significance level α.
8: **else**
9:   B is better than A with confidence level $1 - \epsilon^{min}$ and significance level α.
10: **end if**

In addition, the minimal ϵ for which we can claim, with a confidence level of $1 - \alpha$, that F is almost stochastically dominant over G is:

$$\epsilon^{min}(F_n, G_m, \alpha) = \varepsilon_{W_2}(F_n, G_m) - \sqrt{\frac{n + m}{nm}} \hat{\sigma}_{n,m} \Phi^{-1}(\alpha). \tag{5.11}$$

If $\epsilon^{min}(F_n, G_m, \alpha) < 0.5$, we can claim that algorithm A is better than B, and the lower $\epsilon^{min}(F_n, G_m, \alpha)$ is the greater is the gap between the algorithms. When $\epsilon^{min}(F_n, G_m, \alpha) = 0$, algorithm A is stochastically dominant over B. However, if $\epsilon^{min}(F_n, G_m, \alpha) \geq 0.5$, then F is not almost stochastically larger than G (with confidence level $1 - \alpha$) and hence we should accept the null hypothesis that algorithm A is not superior to algorithm B.

del Barrio et al. [2018] proved that, assuming accurate estimation of $\hat{\sigma}_{n,m}$, it holds that:

$$\epsilon^{min}(F_n, G_m, \alpha) = 1 - \epsilon^{min}(G_m, F_n, \alpha). \tag{5.12}$$

Hence, for a given α value, one of the algorithms will be declared superior, unless $\epsilon^{min}(F_n, G_m, \alpha) = \epsilon^{min}(G_m, F_n, \alpha) = 0.5$.

Notice that the minimal ϵ and the rejection condition of the null hypothesis depend on n and m, the number of scores we have for each algorithm. Hence, for the statistical test to have high statistical power we need to make sure that n and m are big enough.

To summarize, the test for almost stochastic dominance (see Algorithm 5.12) meets the three criteria we defined. This is a test for statistical significance under very minimal assumptions on the distribution from which the performance scores are drawn (criterion (a)). Moreover, it quantifies the gap between the two reference distributions (criterion (c)), which allows it to make decisions even in comparisons where the gap between the superior algorithm and the inferior algorithm is not large (criterion (b)).

5.5   EMPIRICAL ANALYSIS

In this section we demonstrate the potential impact of testing for almost stochastic dominance on the way empirical results of NLP models are analyzed. We use the data of Reimers and Gurevych [2017b][3] and Reimers and Gurevych [2017a].[4] This data contains 510 comparison setups for five common NLP sequence tagging tasks: Part of Speech (POS) tagging with the WSJ corpus [Marcus et al., 1993], syntactic chucking with the CoNLL 2000 data [Sang and Buchholz, 2000], Named Entity Recognition with the CoNLL 2003 data [Sang and De Meulder, 2003], Entity Recognition with the ACE2005 data [Walker et al., 2006], and event detection with the TempEval3 data [UzZaman et al., 2013].

In each setup two leading DNNs, either different architectures or variants of the same model but with different hyper-parameter configurations, are compared across various choices of random seeds and hyper-parameter configurations. The exact details are documented in Reimers and Gurevych [2017a,b].

For each experimental setup, we report the outcome of three alternative comparison methods: collection of statistics (COS), stochastic order (SO), and almost stochastic order (ASO). For COS, we report the mean, standard deviation, and median of the scores for each algorithm, as well as their minimum and maximum values. We consider one algorithm to be superior over another only if both its mean is greater and its standard deviation is smaller. For SO, we employ the U-test as proposed by Reimers and Gurevych [2018], and consider a result significant if $p \leq 0.05$. Finally, for ASO we employ the method of Section 5.4 and report the identity of the superior algorithm along with its ϵ value, using $p \leq 0.01$.

Analysis Structure   We divide our analysis into three cases. In *Case A*, both the COS and the SO approaches indicate that one of the models is superior. In *Case B*, the previous methods reach contradicting conclusions: while COS indicates that one of the algorithms is superior, SO comes insignificant. Finally, in *Case C* both COS and SO are indecisive. In the 510 comparisons we analyze there is no setup where SO was significant but COS could not reach a decision. We start with an example setup for each case and then provide a summary of all 510 comparisons.

Results: Case A   We demonstrate that if algorithm A is stochastically larger than algorithm B then all three methods agree that algorithm A is better than B. As an example setup we analyze the comparison between the NER models of Lample et al. [2016] and Ma and Hovy [2016] when running both algorithms multiple times, changing only the random seed fed into the

---

[3]https://github.com/UKPLab/emnlp2017-bilstm-cnn-crf
[4]Which was generously given to us by the authors.

Table 5.1: NER results (Case A)

	Mean	Standard Deviation	Median	Minimum	Maximum
[Lample et al., 2016]	0.9075	0.2237	0.9080	0.9018	0.9113
[Ma and Hovy, 2016]	0.9056	0.3211	0.9063	0.8853	0.9100

Table 5.2: POS tagging results (Case B)

	Mean	Standard Deviation	Median	Minimum	Maximum
Adam	0.9224	0.0604	0.9319	0.1746	0.9556
RMSprop	0.9190	0.0920	0.9349	0.1420	0.9573

random number generator (41 scores from Lample et al. [2016], 87 scores from Ma and Hovy [2016]). The evaluation measure is F1 score. The collection of statistics for the two models is presented in Table 5.1.

The U-test states that Lample et al. [2016] is stochastically larger than Ma and Hovy [2016] with a p-value of 0.00025. This result is also consistent with the prediction of the COS approach as Lample et al. [2016] is better than Ma and Hovy [2016] both in terms of mean (larger) and standard deviation (smaller). Finally, the minimum ϵ value of the ASO method is 0, which also reflects an SO relationship.

Results: Case B   We demonstrate that if the measures of mean and standard deviation from the COS approach indicate that algorithm A is better than algorithm B but stochastic dominance does not hold, then it also holds that A is almost stochastically larger than B with a small $\epsilon > 0$. As an example case we consider the experiment where the performance of a BiL-STM POS tagger with one of two optimizers, Adam [Kingma and Ba, 2014] (3898 scores) or RMSProp [Hinton et al., 2012] (1822 scores), are compared across various hyper-parameter configurations and random seeds. The evaluation measure is word level accuracy. The COS for the two models is presented in Table 5.2.

The result of the U-test came insignificant with p-value of 0.4562. The COS approach predicts that Adam is the better optimizer as both its mean is larger and its standard deviation is smaller. When comparing between Adam and RMSProp, the ASO method returns an ϵ of 0.0159, indicating that the former is almost stochastically larger than the latter.

We note that decisions with the COS method are challenging as it potentially involves a large number of statistics (five in this analysis). Our decision here is to make the COS prediction based on the mean and the standard deviation of the score distribution, even when according to

Table 5.3: NER Results (Case C)

	Mean	Standard Deviation	Median	Minimum	Maximum
Variational	0.8850	0.0392	0.8896	0.0119	0.9098
No Dropout	0.8772	0.0247	0.8799	0.5547	0.8995

Table 5.4: Results summary over the 510 comparisons of Reimers and Gurevych [2017b]

	% of Comparisons	Average ϵ	ϵ Standard Deviation
Case A	0.98%	0.000	0.000
Case B	48.04%	0.072	0.108
Case C	50.98%	0.202	0.143

other statistics the conclusion might have been different. We consider this ambiguity an inherent limitation of the COS method.

Results: Case C   Finally, we address the case where stochastic dominance does not hold and no conclusions can be drawn from the statistics collection. Our observation is that even in these cases ASO is able to determine which algorithm is better with a reasonable level of confidence. We consider again a BiLSTM architecture, this time for NER, where the comparison is between two dropout policies—no dropout (225 scores) and variational dropout (2599 scores). The evaluation measure is the F1 score and the collection of statistics is presented in Table 5.3.

The U-test came insignificant with a p-value of 0.5. COS is also inconclusive as the mean result of the variational dropout approach is higher, but so also its standard deviation. In this case, looking at the other statistics also gives a mixed picture as the median and max values of the variational approach are higher, but its min value is substantially smaller.

The ASO approach indicates that the no dropout approach is almost stochastically larger, with $\epsilon = 0.0279$. An in-depth consideration supports this decision as the much larger standard deviation and the much smaller minimum of the variational approach are indicators of a skewed score distribution that leaves low certainty about future performance.

Results: Summary   We now turn to a summary of our analysis across the 510 comparisons of Reimers and Gurevych [2017b]. Table 5.4 presents the percentage of comparisons that fall into each category, along with the average and the standard deviation of the ϵ value of ASO for each case (all ASO results are significant with $p \leq 0.01$). Figure 5.1 presents the histogram of these ϵ values in each case.

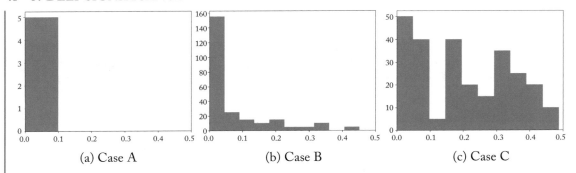

Figure 5.1: Histograms of ϵ values of the ASO method for cases A, B, and C.

The number of comparisons that fall into case A is only 0.98%, indicating that it is rare that a decision about stochastic dominance of one algorithm can be reached when comparing DNNs. We consider this a strong indication that the Mann–Whitney U-test is not suitable for DNN comparison as it has very little statistical power (criterion (b)).

COS makes a decision in 49.01% of the comparisons (case A and B). This method is also somewhat powerful (criterion (b)), but much less so than ASO that is decisive in all 510 comparisons. The ϵ values of ASO are higher for case B than for case A (middle line of Table 5.4, middle graph of Figure 5.1). For case C the ϵ distribution is qualitatively different—ϵ receives a range of values (rightmost graph of Figure 5.1) and its average is 0.202 (bottom line of Table 5.4). We consider this to be a desired behavior as the more complex the picture drawn by COS and SO is, the less confident we expect ASO to be. Being able to make a decision in all 510 comparisons while quantifying the gap between the distributions, we believe that ASO is an appropriate tool for DNN comparison.

5.6   ERROR RATE ANALYSIS

While our extensive analysis indicates the quality of the ASO test, it does not allow us to estimate its false positive and false negative rates. This is because in our 510 comparisons there is no oracle (or gold standard) that says if one of the algorithms is superior. Next, we provide such analyses.

False Positive Rate   The ASO test is defined such that the ε value required for rejecting the conclusion that algorithm A is better than B is defined by the practitioner. While $\varepsilon = 0.5$ indicates a clear rejection, most researchers would probably set a lower ε threshold. Our goal in the next analysis is to present a case where the false positive rate of ASO is very low, even when one refrains from declaring one algorithm as better than the other only when ε is very close to 0.5.

To do that, we consider a scenario where each of the 255 score distributions of the experiments above is compared to a variant of the same distribution after a Gaussian noise with a 0 expectation and a standard deviation of 0.001 is added to each of the scores. Since in all the tasks

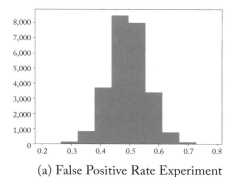

(a) False Positive Rate Experiment

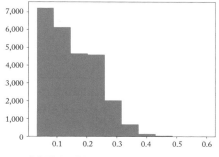

(b) False Negative Rate Experiment

Figure 5.2: Histograms of the ϵ values of the ASO test in the ablation experiments.

we consider the scores are in the $[0, 1]$ range, the value of 0.001 is equivalent to 0.1%. Since the average of the standard deviations of these 255 score distributions is 0.06, our noise is small but not negligible. We choose this relatively small symmetric noise so that with a high probability the original score distribution and the modified one should not be considered different. We run 100 comparisons for each of the 255 algorithms.

We compute the ε such that a value of 0 means that the non-noisy version is better than the noisy one with the strongest confidence, while the value of 1 means the exact opposite (both values are not observed in practice). A value of 0.5 indicates that no algorithm is superior which is the correct prediction.

Figure 5.2 (a) presents a histogram of the ε values. The averaged ε is 0.502 with a standard deviation of 0.0472, and 95% of the ε values are in $[0.396, 0.631]$. This means that if we set a threshold of 0.4 on ε (i.e., lower than 0.4 or higher than 0.6), the false positive rate would be lower than 5%. In comparison, the COS approach declares the noisy version superior in 26.2% of the 255 comparisons, and the non-noisy version in 23.8%: a false positive rate of 50%. The SO test makes no mistakes, as a false positive of this test is equivalent to an ε value of 0 or 1 for ASO.

Another interesting setup is where for each of the 255 algorithms the performance score set is randomly split into two equal sized sets. This simulates a situation where an algorithm is compared to itself and hence we would expect a good evaluation method to deem both algorithms equal. We performed such an experiment, repeating the random split process 100 times for each algorithm, and using ASO to compare between the sets. In all cases we observed an averaged ε of 0.5, indicating that the method avoids false positive predictions when an algorithm is compared to itself.

False Negative Rate   This analysis complements the previous one by demonstrating the low false negative rate of ASO in a case where it is clear that one distribution is better than the other. For each of the 255 score distributions we generate a noisy distribution by randomly splitting the scores into a set A of $\frac{1}{4}$ of the scores and the complementary set $\hat{A}$ of the rest of the scores. For each score s, we sample a noise parameter ϕ from a Gaussian with a 0 expectation and a standard deviation of 0.01, adding to s the value of $(-1) \cdot \phi^2$ if $s \in A$, and ϕ^2 if $s \in \hat{A}$. The noisy distribution is superior to the original one, with a high probability. As before we perform 100 comparisons for each of the 255 algorithms.

We compute ε such that a value of 0 would mean that the noisy version is superior. The ε values are plotted in Figure 5.2 (b): their average is 0.134, standard deviation is 0.07 and more than 99% of the values are lower than 0.4 (the same threshold as in the first experiment). The COS test deems the noisy distribution superior in 87.4% of the cases, while in the rest it considers none of the distributions superior. SO has a false negative rate of 100% as $\varepsilon > 0$ in all experiments.

5.7   SUMMARY

DNNs have made a substantial contribution to NLP. Indeed, the state of the art of almost every supervised NLP task has been improved in the past few years based on this technology. As expected, ground breaking solutions come with a paradigm shift and in this case one of the main changes DNNs bring to NLP is the transfer from convex, deterministic models to non-convex, non-deterministic alternatives. Naturally, such a radical shift is inherently tied to unique evaluation challenges.

In this chapter we have proposed an evaluation framework for non-deterministic machine learning algorithms like DNNs, and made a concrete proposal for an evaluation method that obeys the criteria defined by our proposed framework. While we see the proposed framework and the derived evaluation method as a natural extension of the hypothesis testing framework of Chapter 2, we recognize that this is only an initial attempt to deal with this problem from a rigorous statistical viewpoint. Naturally, more research is required in order to evaluate the practical value of our proposal. Moreover, we hope that statistically sound evaluation of non-deterministic models will be further researched by the community so that agreed standards will be reached.

CHAPTER 6

Replicability Analysis

In the previous chapters, we have discussed statistical significance testing in the world of NLP, connected between evaluation metrics and the suitable significance tests, and presented the selection process in a simplified version of a relatively intuitive decision tree. Following, we extended our discussion to statistically sound comparison between non-deterministic models such as DNNs. However, we have only addressed the use of **one dataset** per comparison. Nowadays, with the ever-growing amount of textual data from various languages, domains, and genres, evaluating NLP algorithms on multiple datasets has become a standard, as such a multitude of tests ensures a consistent performance across heterogeneous setups.

A problem arises when one tries to apply the standard hypothesis testing framework to multiple comparisons, i.e., comparisons across multiple datasets. For example, consider a researcher trying to prove the superiority of their proposed algorithm over another on 10 different data sources, naturally seeking for a statistically significant result. If their experiments show that their algorithm does perform better on all 10 datasets, when for each dataset the probability that the experimental result does not represent the actual state of affairs on the experimental domain is lower than 5%, then the true probability of the algorithm being superior in all 10 domains is only $0.95^{10} = 0.598$.

These *multiple comparisons* pose a true challenge to traditional statistical testing methods such as those we have described, and using them in the traditional setup can therefore lead to erroneous conclusions. In this chapter we will address this challenge and present a *Replicability Analysis* framework for a statistically sound analysis of multiple comparisons, i.e., comparisons across different datasets. Replicability analysis, is often referred to as the cornerstone of science [Moonesinghe et al., 2007]. It is of predominant importance in many scientific fields including psychology [Open Science Collaboration, 2012], genomics [Heller et al., 2014], economics [Herndon et al., 2014], and medicine [Begley and Ellis, 2012], among others. Findings are usually considered as replicated if they are obtained in two or more studies that differ from each other in some aspects, e.g., language, domain, or genre in NLP.

6.1 THE MULTIPLICITY PROBLEM

Written language is now, perhaps for the first time in human history, a common and cheap resource. With the Web providing us vast amounts of text in multiple languages, domains, and genres, it is natural that the expectations from NLP algorithms grow as well. Indeed, evaluating a new algorithm on as many languages, domains, and genres as possible is becoming a de-facto standard. While only a decade ago it was customary to evaluate an algorithm on a single dataset from a single domain, it is not rare these days to see NLP papers with evaluation across dozens of datasets.

For example, the phrase structure parsers of Charniak [2000] and Collins [2003] were mostly evaluated on the Wall Street Journal Penn Treebank [Marcus et al., 1993], consisting of written, edited English text of economic news. During the first decade of the century multilingual evaluation has become an actual standard for dependency parsing, with the introduction of the CoNLL 2006–2007 shared tasks on multilingual dependency parsing [Buchholz and Marsi, 2006, Nilsson et al., 2007], consisting of corpora in 19 languages. During the last decade, the Universal Dependency Bank [Nivre et al., 2016] with dozens of languages and multiple corpora in many of them, has been adopted as a new evaluation standard, and additional challenges, such as the shared task on parsing multiple English Web domains [Petrov and McDonald, 2012] are continuously proposed.

While the number of evaluation tasks grows, the statistical analysis toolbox employed by NLP researchers has remained quite traditional. Indeed, in most experimental NLP papers, several algorithms are compared on a number of datasets where the performance of each algorithm is reported together with per-dataset statistical significance figures. However, with the growing number of evaluation datasets, it becomes more challenging to draw comprehensive conclusions from such comparisons. This is due to an intuitive, yet highly important fact—although the probability of drawing an erroneous conclusion from a single comparison is small, with multiple comparisons the probability of making one or more false claims may be very high. With this challenge in mind, in this chapter we present a statistical analysis framework commonly referred to as replicability analysis, that allows researchers to draw statistically sound conclusions in evaluation setups that involve multiple comparisons.

The classical goal of replicability analysis is to examine the consistency of findings across studies in order to address the basic dogma of science that a finding is more convincingly true if it is replicated in at least one more study [Heller et al., 2014, Patil et al., 2016]. We adapt this goal to NLP, where we aim to ascertain the superiority of one algorithm over another across multiple datasets, differentiated by languages, domains, or genres. Finding that one algorithm outperforms another across domains gives a sense of consistency to the results and positive evidence that the better performance is not specific to a selected setup.

"Replicability" is sometimes referred to as "reproducibility". In recent NLP work the term reproducibility was used when trying to get identical results on the same data [Marrese-Taylor and Matsuo, 2017, Névéol et al., 2016]. Here we adopt the meaning of "replicability" and its distinction from "reproducibility" from Peng [2011] and Leek and Peng [2015] and refer to replicability analysis as the effort to show that a finding is consistent over different datasets from different domains or languages, and is not idiosyncratic to a specific scenario. In this discussion we are particularly interested in two questions.

1. *Counting:* For how many datasets does a given algorithm outperform another?

2. *Identification:* What are these datasets?

Notice that experimental NLP papers usually answer these exact two questions. In some cases, this is done without any statistical analysis, by simply declaring better performance of a given algorithm for datasets on which its performance measure is better than that of the algorithm it is compared to. In other cases decisions are based on the *p*-values from statistical tests performed independently on each dataset: declaring better performance for datasets with *p*-value below a pre-defined significance level, e.g., 0.05. While the first approach is clearly not statistically valid, the second approach, which may seem statistically sound, is not valid as well (see the discussion in the beginning of this chapter). These approaches may lead to erroneous conclusions that could result in adopting new (and probably complicated) algorithms, which are in fact not better than the previous (probably simpler) ones. To formalize the above discussion, we will later demonstrate that the current comparison practice does not guarantee to bound the probability to make at least one erroneous claim, even when statistical significance testing is properly performed (see Section 6.2). The unavoidable conclusion is that this approach is error-prone when the number of participating datasets is large.

In this chapter we hence present an alternative approach. For question (1), we discuss the approach of Benjamini et al. [2009] for replicability analysis of multiple studies, which is based on the partial conjunction framework of Benjamini and Heller [2008]. This analysis comes with a guarantee that the probability of overestimating the true number of datasets with effect, i.e., the datasets in which a significant difference was displayed, is upper bounded by a predefined constant. For question (2), we motivate a multiple testing procedure which guarantees that the probability of making at least one erroneous claim on the superiority of one algorithm over another is upper bounded by a predefined constant.

This framework could potentially increase the number of standard evaluation setups per task when appropriate (e.g., experimenting on additional languages and domains), possibly paving the way to hundreds of comparisons per study. This is due to two main reasons. First, this is a statistically sound framework that allows researchers to safely draw valid conclusions with well defined statistical guarantees. Second, this framework provides means of summarizing a large number of experiments with a handful of easily interpretable numbers (see Table 6.1). This allows researchers to report results over a large number of comparisons in a concise manner, delving into details of particular comparisons when necessary.

Before delving into the proposed framework, let us touch upon two important points. First, we wish to present several representative examples for multiple comparisons in NLP, focusing on evaluations across multiple languages and multiple domains. Second, we discuss existing analysis frameworks for multiple comparisons, both in the NLP and in the machine learning literatures, pointing to the need for establishing new standards for our community.

Multiple Comparisons in NLP   Multiple comparisons of algorithms over datasets from different languages, domains, and genres have become a de-facto standard in many areas of NLP. A common multilingual example is, naturally, machine translation, where it is customary to compare algorithms across a large number of source-target language pairs. This is done, for example, with the Europarl corpus consisting of 21 European languages [Koehn, 2005, Koehn and Schroeder, 2007] and with the datasets of the WMT workshop series with its multiple domains (e.g., news and biomedical in 2017), each consisting of several language pairs (7 and 14, respectively, in 2017). Multiple dataset comparisons are also abundant in domain adaptation work. Representative tasks include named entity recognition [Guo et al., 2009], POS tagging [Daumé, 2007], dependency parsing [Petrov and McDonald, 2012], word sense disambiguation [Chan and Ng, 2007], and sentiment classification [Blitzer et al., 2007, 2006].

More recently, with the emergence of crowd-sourcing platforms that make data collection quick and financially convenient [Snow et al., 2008], an ever-growing number of datasets is being created. This is apparent in all NLP domains, but is particularly noticeable in lexical semantics tasks that have become central in NLP research due to the prominence of neural networks. For example, it is customary to compare word embedding models [Levy and Goldberg, 2014, Mikolov et al., 2013, Ó Séaghdha and Korhonen, 2014, Pennington et al., 2014, Schwartz et al., 2015] on multiple datasets where word pairs are scored according to the degree to which different semantic relations, such as similarity and association, hold between the members of the pair [Bruni et al., 2014, Finkelstein et al., 2001, Hill et al., 2015, Silberer and Lapata, 2014]. In some works (e.g., Baroni et al. [2014]) these embedding models are compared across a large number of simple tasks. Another recent popular example is work on compositional distributional semantics and sentence embedding. For example, Wieting et al. [2016] compare 6 sentence representation models on no less than 24 task.

The results from each dataset are usually presented in a comparison table and the statistically significant differences are marked. However, the tests usually applied for statistical evaluation in NLP are compatible only for a comparison made on a **single dataset**, i.e., it is not statistically valid to count the number of significant results and report them, since the actual number of significant outcomes can be much smaller in reality.

Existing Analysis Frameworks   Machine learning work on multiple dataset comparisons dates back to Dietterich [1998] who raised the question: "given two learning algorithms and datasets from several domains, which algorithm will produce more accurate classifiers when trained on examples from new domains?" Demšar [2006] proposed practical means for this problem: Given performance measures for two algorithms on multiple datasets, the authors test whether there is at least one dataset on which the difference between the algorithms is statistically significant. For this goal they propose methods such as a paired t-test, a nonparametric sign-rank test and a wins/losses/ties count, where all these are computed across results collected from all participating datasets. However, their methods are designed only to respond to the binary question about which algorithm is superior. In contrast, we wish to count and identify the datasets for which one algorithm significantly outperforms the other, a method that will provide more intricate information, especially when the datasets come from vastly different sources.

In NLP, several papers have addressed the problem of measuring the statistical significance of results on a single dataset (e.g., Berg-Kirkpatrick et al. [2012]; Søgaard [2013]; Søgaard et al. [2014]). To the best of our knowledge, Søgaard [2013] is the only work that addressed the statistical properties of evaluation with multiple datasets. For this aim they modified the statistical tests proposed in Demšar [2006] to use a Gumbel distribution assumption on the test statistics, which they considered to suit NLP better than the original Gaussian assumption. However, while this procedure aims to estimate the effect size across datasets, it answers neither the counting nor the identification question.

Now that we have discussed the preliminaries of the multiplicity problem and briefly surveyed relevant previous work, we are ready to present a multiple hypothesis testing framework.

6.2   A MULTIPLE HYPOTHESIS TESTING FRAMEWORK FOR ALGORITHM COMPARISON

Let us begin by revisiting the formulation of a general hypothesis testing framework for a comparison between two algorithms, similar to that which has been presented in Chapter 2. This framework will help up develop our ideas.

We wish to compare between two algorithms, A and B. Let X be a collection of datasets $X = \{X^1, X^2, \ldots, X^N\}$, where for all $i \in \{1, \ldots, N\}$, $X^i = \{x_{i,1}, \ldots, x_{i,n_i}\}$.

$$
X = \left\{
\begin{array}{rl}
X^1 = & \left(x_{1,1}, \ldots, x_{1,n_1}\right), \\
X^2 = & \left(x_{2,1}, \ldots, x_{2,n_2}\right), \\
\vdots & \qquad \vdots \\
X^n = & \left(x_{n,1}, \ldots, x_{n,n_n}\right)
\end{array}
\right\}.
$$

Each dataset X^i can be of a different language or a different domain. We denote by $x_{i,k}$ the granular unit on which results are being measured, that, in most NLP tasks, is a word or a sequence of words. The difference in performance between the two algorithms is measured using one or more of the evaluation measures in the set $\mathcal{M} = \{\mathcal{M}_1, \ldots, \mathcal{M}_m\}$.[1]

Let us denote $\mathcal{M}_j(ALG, X^i)$ as the value of the measure $\mathcal{M}_j$ when algorithm ALG is applied on the dataset X^i. Without loss of generality, we assume that higher values of the measure are better. We define the difference in performance between two algorithms, A and B, according to the measure $\mathcal{M}_j$ on the dataset X^i as:

$$
\delta_j\left(X^i\right) = \mathcal{M}_j\left(A, X^i\right) - \mathcal{M}_j\left(B, X^i\right). \tag{6.1}
$$

---

[1]For now, let us assume that only one evaluation measure is used. Our framework can be easily extended to deal with multiple measures.

Finally, using this notation we formulate the following statistical hypothesis testing problem:

$$H_{0i}(j) : \delta_j\left(X^i\right) \leq 0$$
$$H_{1i}(j) : \delta_j\left(X^i\right) > 0.$$

(6.2)

The null hypothesis, stating that there is no difference between the performance of algorithm A and algorithm B, or that B performs better, is tested vs. the alternative statement that A is superior. If the statistical test results in rejecting the null hypothesis, one concludes that A outperforms B in this setup. Otherwise, there is not enough evidence in the data to make this conclusion.

As we previously discussed, rejection of the null hypothesis when it is true is termed *type* I *error*, and non rejection of the null hypothesis when the alternative is true is termed *type* II *error*. Ideally, one would like to minimize the probability of both error types. Unfortunately, reducing the probability of one of the errors often causes an increase in the probability of the other error. The classical approach to hypothesis testing is to find a test that guarantees that the probability of making a type I error is upper bounded by a predefined constant α, the test significance level, while achieving as low probability of type II error as possible, a.k.a achieving as high power as possible.

This formulation addresses the comparison between two algorithms on a single dataset, X. We next turn to the case where the difference between two algorithms is tested across multiple datasets: $X = \{X^1, X^2, \ldots, X^N\}$. This multiplicity in datasets creates a reality of multiple hypotheses.

With more datasets comes more responsibility. If N is large, testing each hypothesis separately at the nominal significance level may result in a high number of erroneously rejected null hypotheses. In our context, when the performance of algorithm A is compared to that of algorithm B across multiple datasets, and for each dataset algorithm A is declared as superior, based on a statistical test at the nominal significance level α, the expected number of erroneous claims may grow as N grows.

For example, if a single test is applied with a significance level of $\alpha = 0.05$, there is only a 5% chance of incorrectly rejecting the null hypothesis. On the other hand, for 100 tests where all null hypotheses are true, the expected number of incorrect rejections is $100 \cdot 0.05 = 5$. Denoting the total number of type I errors as V, we can see below that if the test statistics are independent then the probability of making at least one incorrect rejection is 0.994:

$$\mathbb{P}(V > 0) = 1 - \mathbb{P}(V = 0) =$$
$$1 - \prod_{i=1}^{100} \mathbb{P}(\text{no type I error in } i) = 1 - (1 - 0.05)^{100}.$$

This demonstrates that the naive method of counting the datasets for which significance was reached at the nominal level is error-prone.

The multiple testing literature proposes various procedures for bounding the probability of making at least one type I error, as well as other, less restrictive error criteria (a full survey is presented in Farcomeni [2007]). Our approach, however, addresses the questions of counting and identifying the datasets for which algorithm A outperforms B, with certain statistical guarantees regarding erroneous claims. While identifying the datasets gives more information when compared to just declaring their number, we consider these two questions separately.

We next present the fundamentals of the partial conjunction framework, and start by reformulating the set of hypothesis testing problems of Equation (6.2) as a unified hypothesis testing problem. This framework aims to identify whether algorithm A is superior to B across **all datasets** on which the two are compared. The notation for the null hypothesis in this problem is $H_0^{N/N}$ since we test if N out of N alternative hypotheses are true:

$$H_0^{N/N} : \bigcup_{i=1}^{N} H_{0i} \text{ is true} \quad \text{vs.} \quad H_1^{N/N} : \bigcap_{i=1}^{N} H_{1i} \text{ is true}. \tag{6.3}$$

Requiring the rejection of the disjunction of all null hypotheses is often too restrictive for it involves observing a significant effect on all datasets, $i \in \{1, \dots, N\}$. Instead, one can require a rejection of the *global null hypothesis* stating that all individual null hypotheses are true, i.e., evidence that at least one alternative hypothesis is true. This hypothesis testing problem is formulated as follows:

$$H_0^{1/N} : \bigcap_{i=1}^{N} H_{0i} \text{ is true} \quad \text{vs.} \quad H_1^{1/N} : \bigcup_{i=1}^{N} H_{1i} \text{ is true}. \tag{6.4}$$

Obviously, rejecting the global null may not provide enough information: it only indicates that algorithm A outperforms B on at least one dataset. Hence, this claim does not give any evidence for the consistency of the results across multiple datasets. A natural compromise between the above two formulations is to test the *partial conjunction null*, which states that the number of false null hypotheses is lower than u, where $1 \leq u \leq N$ is a pre-specified integer constant. The *partial conjunction test* contrasts this statement with the alternative statement that at least u out of the N null hypotheses are false.

Definition 6.1 [Benjamini and Heller, 2008]. Consider $N \geq 2$ null hypotheses: $H_{01}, H_{02}, \dots, H_{0N}$, and let $p_1, \dots, p_N$ be their associated p-values. Let k be the true unknown number of false null hypotheses, then our question "Are at least u out of N null hypotheses false?" can be formulated as follows:

$$H_0^{u/N} : k < u \quad \text{vs.} \quad H_1^{u/N} : k \geq u. \tag{6.5}$$

In our context, the partial conjunction hypothesis testing examines if algorithm A outperforms B in at least u out of n datasets, and k is the number of domains or languages for which algorithm A **is truly better**. Following this definition, Benjamini and Heller [2008] explained why partial conjunction testing may be more adequate than testing the global null in the context of genetic studies. This also applies to NLP since we do not solely want to know if a given algorithm is superior on at least one dataset, but instead we wish to establish the differences between the compared algorithms across a variety of languages and domains. In the next section we further elaborate on partial conjunction testing for our purposes.

6.3   REPLICABILITY ANALYSIS WITH PARTIAL CONJUNCTION TESTING

The replicability analysis framework we propose here [Benjamini and Heller, 2008, Benjamini et al., 2009] is based on partial conjunction testing. Particularly, these authors have shown that a lower bound on the number of false null hypotheses with a confidence level of $1 - \alpha$ can be obtained by finding the largest u for which we can reject the partial conjunction null hypothesis $H_0^{u/N}$ along with $H_0^{1/N}, \ldots, H_0^{(u-1)/N}$ at a significance level α. Since rejecting $H_0^{u/N}$ means that we see evidence in at least u out of N datasets, algorithm A is superior to B. This lower bound on k is taken as our answer to the counting question that we have raised in the beginning of this chapter.

In line with the hypothesis testing framework of Section 6.2, the partial conjunction null, $H_0^{u/N}$, is rejected at level α if $p^{u/N} \leq \alpha$, where $p^{u/N}$ is the partial conjunction p-value. Based on the known methods for testing the global null hypothesis (see, e.g., Loughin [2004]), Benjamini and Heller [2008] proposed methods for combining the p-values $p_1, \ldots, p_N$ of $H_{01}, H_{02}, \ldots, H_{0N}$ in order to obtain $p^{u/N}$.

The methods we focus on were developed by Benjamini and Heller [2008], and are based on Fisher's and Bonferroni's methods for testing the global null hypothesis. For brevity, we name them *Bonferroni* and *Fisher*. We choose them because they are valid in different setups that are frequently encountered in NLP: Bonferroni for dependent datasets and both Fisher and Bonferroni for independent datasets. The question of which datasets are dependent and which are independent is far from being trivial. For simplicity, we assume that datasets and their corresponding test statistics are independent if the datasets do not have mutual samples, and one dataset is not a transformation of the other.

Even with the above simplifying assumption, in the NLP domain it is often hard to determine the type of dependency between different datasets. Are two datasets in the same language necessarily dependant? How about two datasets constructed by the same researcher? One advantage in Bonferroni's method is that it does not make any assumptions about the dependencies between the participating datasets. In contrast, Fisher's method, while assuming independence across the participating datasets, is often more powerful than Bonferroni's method or other methods which make the same independence assumption (see Loughin [2004] and Benjamini and Heller [2008] for other methods and a comparison between them). We hence focus on the Bonferroni's method for cases where the datasets are dependent and of the more powerful Fisher's method when the datasets are independent.

Let $p_{(i)}$ be the ith smallest p-value among $p_1, \ldots, p_N$. The partial conjunction p-values are:

$$p_{Bonferroni}^{u/N} = (N - u + 1)p_{(u)} \tag{6.6}$$

$$p_{Fisher}^{u/N} = \mathbb{P}\left(\chi_{2(N-u+1)}^2 \geq -2\sum_{i=u}^{N} \ln p_{(i)}\right), \tag{6.7}$$

where $\chi_{2(N-u+1)}^2$ denotes a Chi-squared random variable with $2(N - u + 1)$ degrees of freedom. For each of these methods we reject the partial conjunction null $H_0^{u/n}$ at level α if $p^{u/n} \leq \alpha$.

To understand the reasoning behind these methods, let us consider first the above p-values for testing the global null, i.e., for the case of $u = 1$. Rejecting the global null hypothesis requires evidence that at least one null hypothesis is false. Intuitively, we would like to see one or more small p-values.

Both of the methods above agree with this intuition. Bonferroni's method rejects the global null if $p_{(1)} \leq \alpha/N$, i.e., if the minimum p-value is small enough, where the threshold guarantees that the significance level of the test is α for any dependency among the p-values $p_1, \ldots, p_N$. Fisher's method rejects the global null for large values of $-2\sum_{i=1}^{N} \ln p_{(i)}$, or equivalently for small values of $\prod_{i=1}^{N} p_i$. That is, while both these methods are intuitive, they are different. Fisher's method requires a small enough product of p-values as evidence that at least one null hypothesis is false. Bonferroni's method, on the other hand, requires as evidence at least one small enough p-value.

Now let us consider testing the partial conjunction hypothesis for $u > 1$. If the alternative is true, i.e., at least u null hypotheses are false, then one will find one or more false null hypotheses in any subset of $n - u + 1$ hypotheses. Thus, in order to see evidence that the alternative is true, it is intuitive to require rejection of the global null (the intersection hypothesis) for all subsets of $n - u + 1$ hypotheses.

Both Bonferroni's and Fisher's methods agree with this intuition. It is easy to see that the partial conjunction p-value based on Bonferroni's method is the maximal global null p-value among all the Bonferroni's global null p-values for subsets of $n - u + 1$ hypotheses.

The p-value in Equation (6.6) is below α if for every subset of $n - u + 1$ hypotheses the Bonferroni's global null p-value is below α hence the global null is rejected at the significance level of α for every subset of $n - u + 1$ hypotheses.

Similarly, Fisher's method rejects $H_0^{u/n}$ if for all subsets of $n - u + 1$ null hypotheses, the Fisher's global null p-value is below α.

For the case of $u = N$, i.e., when the alternative states that all null hypotheses are false, both methods require that the maximal p-value is small enough for rejection of $H_0^{N/N}$. This is also intuitive because we expect that all the p-values will be small when all the null hypotheses are false. For other cases, where $1 < u < N$, the reasoning is more complicated and is beyond the scope of this discussion.

The partial conjunction test for a specific u answers the question "Does algorithm A perform better than B on at least u datasets?" Our next step is therefore the estimation of the number of datasets for which algorithm A performs better than B.

6.4   REPLICABILITY ANALYSIS: COUNTING

Recall that the number of datasets where algorithm A outperforms algorithm B (denoted with k in Definition 6.1) is the true number of false null hypotheses in our problem. Benjamini and Heller [2008] proposed to estimate k to be the largest u for which $H_0^{u/N}$, along with $H_0^{1/N}, \ldots, H_0^{(u-1)/N}$ is rejected.

Specifically, the estimator $\hat{k}$ is defined as follows:

$$\hat{k} = \max \left\{ u : p_*^{u/N} \leq \alpha \right\}, \tag{6.8}$$

where $p_*^{u/N} = \max\{p_*^{(u-1)/N}, p^{u/N}\}$, $p^{1/N} = p_*^{1/N}$ [2] and α is the desired upper bound on the probability to overestimate the true k. It is guaranteed that $\mathbb{P}(\hat{k} > k) \leq \alpha$ as long as the p-value combination method used for constructing $p^{u/N}$ is valid for the given dependency across the test statistics.[3] When $\hat{k}$ is based on $p_{Bonferroni}^{u/N}$ it is denoted with $\hat{k}_{Bonferroni}$; when it is based on $p_{Fisher}^{u/N}$, it is denoted with $\hat{k}_{Fisher}$.

We now address to computing $\hat{k}$ using Fisher's and Bonferroni's methods given in Section 6.3. We refer to these estimators as $\hat{k}_{Fisher}$ and $\hat{k}_{Bonferroni}$, respectively. A crucial practical consideration, when choosing between $\hat{k}_{Bonferroni}$ and $\hat{k}_{Fisher}$, is the assumed dependency between the datasets. As discussed in Section 6.3, $p_{Fisher}^{u/N}$ is recommended when the participating datasets are assumed to be independent; when this assumption cannot be made, only $p_{Bonferroni}^{u/N}$ is appropriate. As the $\hat{k}$ estimators are based on the respective $p^{u/N}$s, the same considerations hold when choosing between them, that if one can assume that the datasets are independent, then reporting the $\hat{k}_{Fisher}$ estimator should be preferred since its value may often be higher, as discussed in Section 6.3. When independence between the datasets cannot be assumed, $\hat{k}_{Bonferroni}$ is the estimator of choice since it is valid for arbitrary dependency among the p-values.

With the $\hat{k}$ estimators, one can answer the counting question, reporting that algorithm A is better than algorithm B in at least $\hat{k}$ out of N datasets with a confidence level of $1 - \alpha$. Regarding the identification question, a natural approach would be to declare the $\hat{k}$ datasets with the smallest p-values as those for which the effect holds. However, with $\hat{k}_{Fisher}$ this approach

---

[2]The monotonicity transformation of the p-values is required for controlling the probability to overestimate k. For more details, see Benjamini and Heller [2008].

[3]This result is a special case of Theorem 4 in Benjamini and Heller [2008].

does not guarantee control over type I errors. In contrast, for $\hat{k}_{Bonferroni}$, the above approach comes with such guarantees, as described in the next section.

The partial conjunction framework could not assist us in replying on the second question of identifying these datasets while preserving the statistical validity of the conclusions, hence, to answer this question, we adapt a complementary approach for the multiplicity problem which considers the original set of hypotheses $H_{01}, \ldots, H_{0n}$ rather than combining them into a single hypothesis.

6.5   REPLICABILITY ANALYSIS: IDENTIFICATION

As demonstrated previously, identifying the datasets with p-value below the nominal significance level and declaring them as those for which algorithm A is better than B may lead to a high number of erroneous claims. One can address this problem with a variety of methods.

Recall that we will be testing our algorithm on N different datasets for a significance level of α on each test. A classical and very simple method for addressing such a setup is named *the Bonferroni correction*, which compensates for the increased probability of making at least one type I error by testing each individual hypothesis at a significance level of $\alpha' = \alpha/N$, for our predefined α and N as the number of hypotheses tested.[4] While Bonferroni's correction is valid for any dependency among the p-values, the probability of detecting an actual effect using this procedure is often very low, because of its strict p-value threshold. To alleviate this issue, we introduce the Holm procedure [Holm, 1979] which is both (a) valid for arbitrary dependencies among the datasets; and (b) more powerful than the Bonferroni correction.

The *Holm procedure* [Holm, 1979] is a simple p-value based procedure that is concordant with the partial conjunction analysis when $p_{Bonferroni}^{u/N}$ is used in that analysis. Importantly for NLP applications, Holm controls the probability of making at least one type I error for any type of dependency between the participating datasets.

Let α be the desired upper bound on the probability that at least one false rejection occurs, let $p_{(1)} \leq p_{(2)} \leq \ldots \leq p_{(N)}$ be the ordered p-values and let the associated hypotheses be $H_{(1)} \ldots H_{(N)}$. The Holm procedure for identifying the datasets with a significant effect is given below.

The output of the Holm procedure is a rejection list of null hypotheses; the corresponding datasets are those we return in response to the identification. Note that the Holm procedure rejects a subset of hypotheses with p-value below α. Each p-value is compared to a threshold which is lower than or equal to α and depends on the number of evaluation datasets N. The dependence of the thresholds on N can be intuitively explained as follows: with more datasets, we have an increased probability to make more mistakes. In other words, the probability of making one or more erroneous claims may increase with N. Therefore, it is only natural that

---

[4]Bonferroni's correction is based on similar considerations as $p_{Bonferroni}^{u/N}$ for $u = 1$. The partial conjunction framework (Section 6.2) extends this idea for other values of u.

Algorithm 6.13 The Holm Procedure

Input : $(p_{(1)}, \ldots, p_{(1)})$—ordered p-values of N hypothesis testing problems.
Output : List of rejected null hypotheses.

1: Let k be the minimal index such that $p_{(k)} > \frac{\alpha}{N+1-k}$.
2: Reject the null hypotheses $H_{(1)} \ldots H_{(k-1)}$ and do not reject $H_{(k)} \ldots H_{(N)}$. If no such k exists, then reject all null hypotheses.

in order to bound this probability by a pre-specified level α, the thresholds for p-values should depend on N.

It can be shown that the Holm procedure at level α always rejects the $\hat{k}_{Bonferroni}$ hypotheses with the smallest p-values, where $\hat{k}_{Bonferroni}$ is the lower bound for k with a confidence level of $1 - \alpha$. Therefore, the $\hat{k}_{Bonferroni}$ corresponding to a confidence level of $1 - \alpha$ is always smaller or equal to the number of datasets for which the difference between the compared algorithms is significant at level α. This is not surprising in view of the fact that, without making any assumptions on the dependencies among the datasets, $\hat{k}_{Bonferroni}$ guarantees that the probability of making an overly optimistic claim ($\hat{k} > k$) is bounded by α, when simply counting the number of datasets with p-value below α, the probability of making a too optimistic claim may be close to 1, as demonstrated in Section 6.6.

Other methods for adjusting to multiplicity have been proposed throughout the years, for example the Šidák procedure [Šidák, 1967]. However, they all make assumptions about the dependency between the hypotheses that are hard to verify in the case of NLP data.

Framework Summary

1. Answer to the counting question: calculate $\hat{k} = \max\{u : p_*^{u/N} \le \alpha\}$ of Equation (6.8) with $p_*^{u/N} = \max\{p_*^{(u-1)/N}, p^{u/N}\}$ where

   • $p^{u/N} = p_{Fisher}^{u/N} = \mathbb{P}\left(\chi_{2(N-u+1)}^2 \ge -2\sum_{i=u}^{N} \ln p_{(i)}\right)$ from Equation (6.7) when all datasets can be assumed to be independent or

   • $p^{u/N} = p_{Bonferroni}^{u/N} = (N - u + 1)p_{(u)}$ from Equation (6.6) when such an independence assumption cannot be made.

2. Answer to the identification question: report the rejection list returned by the Holm procedure in Algorithm 6.13.

Our proposed framework is based on certain assumptions regarding the experiments conducted in NLP setups. The most prominent of these assumptions states that for dependent datasets the type of dependency cannot be determined. Indeed, to the best of our knowledge, the nature of the dependency between dependent test sets in NLP work has not been analyzed before. In Chapter 7, we revisit our assumptions and point to alternative methods for answering our questions. These methods may be appropriate under other assumptions that may become relevant in future.

In the following section we demonstrate the value of the proposed replicability analysis through examples utilizing synthetic data, and later on show a similar analysis of state-of-the-art algorithms for four major NLP applications. In our experiments, our point of reference is the standard, yet statistically unjustified, counting method that sets its estimator, $\hat{k}_{count}$, to the number of datasets for which the difference between the compared algorithms is significant with p-value $\leq \alpha$ (i.e., $\hat{k}_{count} = \#\{i : p_i \leq \alpha\}$).[5]

6.6   SYNTHETIC EXPERIMENTS

Rationale   In this section we report a series of experiments with synthetic data. The goal of these experiments is to demonstrate the inherent limitations of the current multiple comparison practice in the NLP literature, to which we refer as the counting method. We also aim to demonstrate the efficacy of the replicability framework discussed above in compensating for these limitations. Notice that in the following experiments we do not aim to generate datasets with language related properties or to simulate real-world NLP experiments. Instead, this is kept to the next section. The main advantage of synthetic data experiments is that they allow clean and more rigorous analysis of focused and well-controlled phenomena.

Experiments   We emulate a test with $N = 100$ hypotheses (for example, 100 different domains or languages) by synthesizing p-values and setting α to be 0.05. We begin with a simulation of a scenario in which algorithm A is equivalent to B for each domain, and the datasets representing these domains are independent. We sample the 100 p-values from a standard uniform distribution, which is the p-value distribution under the null hypothesis, repeating the simulation 1,000 times.

Since all the null hypotheses are true then k, the number of false null hypotheses, is 0. We compute the $\hat{k}_{Bonferroni}$ and $\hat{k}_{Fisher}$ estimators, and compare to $\hat{k}_{count}$. Figure 6.1 presents the histogram of $\hat{k}$ values from all 1,000 iterations according to $\hat{k}_{Bonferroni}$, $\hat{k}_{Fisher}$, and $\hat{k}_{count}$.

The figure clearly demonstrates that $\hat{k}_{count}$ provides an overestimation of k while both $\hat{k}_{Bonferroni}$ and $\hat{k}_{Fisher}$ do much better. This synthetic experiment yields the following probability estimates: while in the count method, we see $\hat{P}(\hat{k}_{count} > k) = 0.963$ which is a gross overestimation, our proposed estimators are $\hat{P}(\hat{k}_{Bonferroni} > k) = 0.001$, $\hat{P}(\hat{k}_{Fisher} > k) = 0.021$ (both

---

[5]We use α in two different contexts: the significance level of an individual test and the bound on the probability to overestimate k. This is the standard notation in the statistical literature.

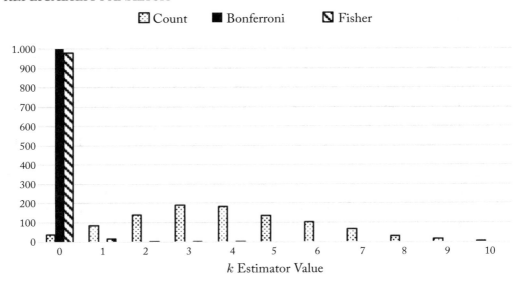

Figure 6.1: $\hat{k}$ histogram in the independent datasets simulation.

lower than 0.05). This simulation strongly supports the theoretical results of the previous sections.

To consider a scenario where there is a dependency between the participating datasets, we consider a second synthetic example. Again we consider $N = 100$ hypotheses (or domains), and generate 100 p-values corresponding to 34 independent normal test statistics, and two other groups of 33 positively correlated normal test statistics with $\rho = 0.2$ and $\rho = 0.5$, respectively. We again assume that all null hypotheses are true and thus all the p-values are distributed uniformly, repeating the simulation 1,000 times. To generate positively dependent p-values, we followed the process described in Section 6.1 of Benjamini et al. [2006].

We estimate the probability that $\hat{k} > k = 0$ for the three $\hat{k}$ estimators based on the 1000 repetitions and get the values of: $\hat{P}(\hat{k}_{count} > k) = 0.943$, $\hat{P}(\hat{k}_{Bonferroni} > k) = 0.046$ and $\hat{P}(\hat{k}_{Fisher} > k) = 0.234$. This simulation demonstrates the importance of using Bonferroni's method rather than Fisher's method when the datasets are dependent, even if some of the datasets are independent. We address the more realistic case, in which not all null hypotheses are false, in the following section with real-world NLP data.

6.7   REAL-WORLD DATA APPLICATIONS

In this section we demonstrate the potential impact of replicability analysis on the way experimental results are analyzed in NLP setups. We explore four NLP applications: (a) two where the datasets are independent: multi-domain dependency parsing and multilingual POS tagging;

and (b) two where dependency between the datasets does exist: cross-domain sentiment classification and word similarity prediction with word embedding models. For each example, we calculated the p-values for each dataset using the adequate statistical test for each task. We next present different types of tasks and appropriate datasets for our experiments.

6.7.1   APPLICATIONS AND DATA

Dependency Parsing   We consider a multi-domain setup, analyzing the results reported in Choi et al. [2015]. The authors compared ten state-of-the-art parsers from which we pick three: (a) Mate[6] [Bohnet, 2010] that performed best on the majority of datasets; (b) Redshift[7] [Honnibal et al., 2013] which demonstrated comparable, still somewhat lower, performance compared to Mate; and (c) SpaCy [Honnibal and Johnson, 2015] that was substantially outperformed by Mate.

All parsers were trained and tested on the English portion of the OntoNotes 5 corpus [Pradhan et al., 2013, Weischedel et al., 2011], a large multi-genre corpus consisting of the following seven genres: broadcasting conversations (BC), broadcasting news (BN), news magazine (MZ), newswire (NW), pivot text (PT), telephone conversations (TC), and web text (WB). Train and test set size (in sentences) range from 6672–34,492 and from 280–2327, respectively, (see Table 1 of Choi et al. [2015]). We copy the test set UAS results of Choi et al. [2015] and compute p-values using the data downloaded from `http://amandastent.com/dependable/`.

For the multilingual setup we experiment with the TurboParser [Martins et al., 2010] on all 19 languages of the CoNLL 2006 and 2007 shared tasks on multilingual dependency parsing [Buchholz and Marsi, 2006, Nilsson et al., 2007]. We compare the performance of the first order parser trained with the MIRA algorithm to the same parser when trained with the perceptron algorithm, both implemented within the TurboParser.

POS Tagging   We consider a multilingual setup, analyzing the results reported in Pinter et al. [2017]. The authors compare their MIMICK model with the model of Ling et al. [2015], denoted with CHAR→TAG. Evaluation is performed on 23 of the 44 languages shared by the Polyglot word embedding dataset [Al-Rfou et al., 2013] and the universal dependencies (UD) dataset [De Marneffe et al., 2014]. Pinter et al. [2017] choose their languages so that they reflect a variety of typological, and particularly morphological, properties. The training/test split is the standard UD split. We copy the word level accuracy figures of Pinter et al. [2017] for the low resource training set setup, the focus setup of that paper. The authors kindly sent us their p-values.

Sentiment Classification   In this task, an algorithm is trained on reviews from one domain and should classify the sentiment of reviews from another domain to the positive and negative classes. For replicability analysis we explore the results of Ziser and Reichart [2017] for the

---

[6]`code.google.com/p/mate-tools`
[7]`github.com/syllog1sm/Redshift`

cross-domain sentiment classification task of Blitzer et al. [2007]. The data in this task consists of Amazon product reviews from 4 domains: books (B), DVDs (D), electronic items (E), and kitchen appliances (K), for the total of 12 domain pairs, each domain having a 2000 review test set.[8] Ziser and Reichart [2017] compared the accuracy of their AE-SCL-SR model to MSDA [Chen et al., 2011], a well-known domain adaptation method, and kindly sent us the required *p*-values.

Word Similarity   We compare two state-of-the-art word embedding collections: (a) word2vec CBOW [Mikolov et al., 2013] vectors, generated by the model titled the best "predict" model in Baroni et al. [2014];[9] and (b) GloVe [Pennington et al., 2014] vectors generated by a model trained on a 42 B token common web crawl.[10] We employed the demo of Faruqui and Dyer [2014] to perform a Spearman correlation evaluation of these vector collections on 12 English word pair datasets: WS-353 [Finkelstein et al., 2001], WS-353-SIM [Agirre et al., 2009], WS-353-REL [Agirre et al., 2009], MC-30 [Miller and Charles, 1991], RG-65 [Rubenstein and Goodenough, 1965], Rare-Word [Luong et al., 2013], MEN [Bruni et al., 2012], MTurk-287 [Radinsky et al., 2011], MTurk-771 [Halawi et al., 2012], YP-130 [Yang and Powers, 2006], SimLex-999 [Hill et al., 2015], and Verb-143 [Baker et al., 2014].

6.7.2   STATISTICAL SIGNIFICANCE TESTING

We first calculate the *p*-values for each task and dataset according to the principles of *p*-values computation for NLP as discussed in Chapter 4 of this book. Yet, to be compatible with previous literature on statistical significance testing in NLP, we put a special emphasis on consistency with the tests reported in Yeh [2000], Berg-Kirkpatrick et al. [2012], and Søgaard et al. [2014]. The methods are as follows.

For dependency parsing, we employ the nonparametric paired bootstrap test [Efron and Tibshirani, 1994] that does not assume any distribution on the test statistics. While t-test can be applied to the UAS and LAS evaluation measure, we chose the bootstrap test so that to be in-line with previous work that assumed that the distribution of the values for the measures commonly applied in this task is unknown. We implemented the test as in Berg-Kirkpatrick et al. [2012] with a bootstrap size of 500 and with 10^5 repetitions.

For multilingual POS tagging, we employ the Wilcoxon signed-rank test [Wilcoxon, 1945] on the differences of the sentence level accuracy scores of the two compared models. This test is a nonparametric test for differences in measure, testing the null hypothesis that the difference has a symmetric distribution around zero. It is appropriate for tasks with paired continuous measures for each observation, which is the case when comparing sentence level accuracies. Note that this test is the nonparametric version of Welch's t-test.

---

[8]http://www.cs.jhu.edu/~mdredze/datasets/sentiment
[9]http://clic.cimec.unitn.it/composes/semantic-vectors.html. Parameters: 5-word context window, 10 negative samples, subsampling, 400 dimensions.
[10]http://nlp.stanford.edu/projects/glove/. 300 dimensions.

For sentiment classification we employ the McNemar test for paired nominal data [McNemar, 1947]. This test is appropriate for binary classification tasks and since we compare the results of the algorithms when applied on the same datasets, we employ its paired version. Finally, for word similarity with its Spearman correlation evaluation, we choose the Steiger test [Steiger, 1980] for comparing elements in a correlation matrix (this is a valid alternative to the Z-test recommended in Chapter 4 for such cases).

We consider the case of $\alpha = 0.05$ for all four applications. For the dependent datasets experiments (sentiment classification and word similarity prediction) with their generally lower p-values (see below), we also consider the case where $\alpha = 0.01$.

Notice that many of the models we experiment with are based on DNNs and are hence non-deterministic in nature. Yet, for the current analysis we do not address this non-determinism following our discussion in Chapter 5, but rather consider only the best development data configuration of each DNN. We do so in order to keep our results easy to interpret and discuss. Of course, the two frameworks of replicability (this chapter) and deep significance (Chapter 5) analysis should be used together in order to promise statistically sound evaluation. We leave this for future research.

6.7.3   RESULTS

Table 6.1 summarizes the replicability analysis results while Tables 6.2–6.6 present task specific performance measures (UAS for parsing, accuracy for sentiment classification, and Spearman ρ coefficient with human judgments for word embeddings) and p-values according to the task specific significance tests described above.

Independent Datasets   Dependency parsing (Table 6.2) and multilingual POS tagging (Table 6.3) are our example tasks for this setup, where $\hat{k}_{Fisher}$ is our recommended valid estimator for the number of cases where one algorithm outperforms another. For dependency parsing, we compare two scenarios: (a) where in most domains the differences between the compared algorithms are quite large and the p-values are small (Mate vs. SpaCy); and (b) where in most domains the differences between the compared algorithms are smaller and the p-values are higher (Mate vs. Redshift). Our multilingual POS tagging scenario (MIMICK vs. Char→Tag) is more similar to scenario (b) in terms of the differences between the participating algorithms.

Table 6.1 demonstrates the $\hat{k}$ estimators for the various tasks and scenarios. For dependency parsing, as expected, in scenario (a) where all the p-values are small, all estimators, even the error-prone $\hat{k}_{count}$, provide the same information. In case (b) of dependency parsing, however, $\hat{k}_{Fisher}$ estimates the number of domains where Mate outperforms Redshift to be 5, while $\hat{k}_{count}$ estimates this number to be 2. This is a substantial difference given that the number of domains is 7. The $\hat{k}_{Bonferroni}$ estimator, that is valid under arbitrary dependencies, is even more conservative than $\hat{k}_{count}$ and its estimation is only 1.

Table 6.1: Replicability analysis results. The appropriate estimator for each scenario is in bold. For independent datasets $\alpha = 0.05$. $\hat{k}_{count}$ is based on the current practice in the NLP literature and does not have statistical guarantees regarding overestimation of the true k. Likewise, $\hat{k}_{Fisher}$ does not provide statistical guarantees regarding the overestimation of the true k for dependent datasets.

	$\hat{k}_{count}$	$\hat{k}_{Bonf.}$	$\hat{k}_{Fish.}$
Independent Datasets			
Dependency Parsing (7 datasets)			
Mate-SpaCy	7	7	**7**
Mate-Redshift	2	1	**5**
Multilingual POS Tagging (23 datasets)			
Mimick-Char→Tag	11	6	**16**
Dependent Datasets			
Sentiment Classification (12 setups)			
AE-SCL-SR-MSDA ($\alpha = 0.05$)	10	**6**	10
AE-SCL-SR-MSDA ($\alpha = 0.01$)	6	**2**	8
Word Similarity (12 datasets)			
W2V-GloVe ($\alpha = 0.05$)	8	**6**	7
W2V-GloVe ($\alpha = 0.01$)	6	**4**	6

Table 6.2: UAS results for multi-domain dependency parsing. p-values are in parentheses, the comparison was made between SpaCy/Redshift models and the Mate model.

Domain	Mate	SpaCy	Redshift	p-val Mate-SpaCy	p-val Mate-Redshift
BC	90.73	89.05	90.19	10^{-4}	0.09
BN	90.82	89.31	90.46	10^{-4}	0.16
MZ	91.92	89.29	90.90	0.0	$4 \cdot 10^{-3}$
NW	91.68	89.52	90.99	0.0	0.03
PT	96.64	95.27	96.22	$2 \cdot 10^{-4}$	0.09
TC	89.87	87.65	88.99	$9 \cdot 10^{-4}$	0.09
WB	89.89	87.40	89.31	0.0	0.08

Table 6.3: Multilingual POS tagging accuracy for the MIMICK and the Char→Tag models. *
indicates languages identified by the Holm procedure with $\alpha = 0.05$.

Language	MIMICK	Char→Tag	ρ-Value
Kazakh	83.95	83.64	0.0944
Tamil*	81.55	84.97	0.0001
Latvian	84.32	84.49	0.0623
Vietnamese	84.22	84.85	0.0359
Hungarian*	88.93	85.83	$1.12 \cdot 10^{-08}$
Turkish	85.60	84.23	0.1461
Greek	93.63	94.05	0.0104
Bulgarian	93.16	93.03	0.1957
Swedish	92.30	92.27	0.0939
Basque*	84.44	86.01	$3.87 \cdot 10^{-10}$
Russian	89.72	88.65	0.0081
Danish	90.13	89.96	0.1016
Indonesian*	89.34	89.81	$8 \cdot 10^{-04}$
Chinese*	85.69	81.84	0.0000
Persian	93.58	93.53	0.4450
Hebrew	91.69	91.93	0.1025
Romanian	89.18	88.96	0.2198
English	88.45	88.89	0.0208
Arabic	90.58	90.49	0.0731
Hindi	87.77	87.92	0.0288
Italian	92.50	92.45	0.4812
Spanish	91.41	91.71	0.1176
Czech*	90.81	90.17	$2.91 \cdot 10^{-05}$

Table 6.4: Cross-domain sentiment classification accuracy for models taken from Ziser and Reichart [2017]. In an $X \rightarrow Y$ setup, X is the source domain and Y is the target domain. $*$ and $+$ indicate domains identified by the Holm procedure with $\alpha = 0.05$ and $\alpha = 0.01$, respectively.

Dataset	AE-SCL-SR	MSDA	ρ-Value
$B \rightarrow K$	0.80	0.78	0.0268
$B \rightarrow D^*$	0.81	0.78	0.0011
$B \rightarrow E$	0.76	0.74	0.0119
$K \rightarrow B^*$	0.72	0.70	0.0038
$K \rightarrow D^{*,+}$	0.76	0.71	$1.9 \cdot 10^{-6}$
$K \rightarrow E$	0.84	0.82	0.018
$D \rightarrow B$	0.77	0.76	0.0186
$D \rightarrow K^*$	0.80	0.77	$1.4 \cdot 10^{-3}$
$D \rightarrow E^*$	0.78	0.75	0.0011
$E \rightarrow B$	0.71	0.71	0.4823
$E \rightarrow K$	0.84	0.84	0.9507
$E \rightarrow D^{*,+}$	0.74	0.71	$3 \cdot 10^{-4}$

Perhaps not surprisingly, the multilingual POS tagging results are similar to case (b) of dependency parsing. Here, again, $\hat{k}_{count}$ is too conservative, estimating the number of languages with effect to be 11 (out of 23) while $\hat{k}_{Fisher}$ estimates this number to be 16, an increase of 5/23 in the estimated number of languages with effect. $\hat{k}_{Bonferroni}$ is again more conservative, estimating the number of languages with effect to be only 6, which is not very surprising given that it does not exploit the independence between the datasets. These two examples of case (b) demonstrate that when the differences between the algorithms are quite small, $\hat{k}_{Fisher}$ may be more sensitive than the current practice in NLP for discovering the number of datasets with effect.

To complete the analysis, we would like to name the datasets with effect. As discussed Section 6.1, while this can be straightforwardly done by naming the datasets with the $\hat{k}$ smallest p-values, in general, this approach does not control the probability of identifying at least one dataset erroneously. We thus employ the Holm procedure for the identification task, noticing that the number of datasets it identifies should be equal to the value of the $\hat{k}_{Bonferroni}$ estimator (see Section 6.5).

Indeed, for dependency parsing in case (a), the Holm procedure identifies all seven domains as cases where Mate outperforms SpaCy, while in case (b) it identifies only the MZ domain as a case where Mate outperforms Redshift. For multilingual POS tagging the Holm procedure identifies Tamil, Hungarian, Basque, Indonesian, Chinese, and Czech as languages

Table 6.5: UAS results for multilingual dependency parsing

Language	MIRA	Perceptron	ρ-Value
Arabic	84.93	73.98	0.0000
Basque	82.18	81.03	0.0000
Bulgarian	93.51	92.55	0.0000
Catalan	93.36	92.46	0.0000
Chinese	87.86	86.93	0.0064
Czech	87.40	85.73	0.0000
Danish	90.17	89.31	$8 \cdot 10^{-5}$
Dutch	87.57	87.03	0.0159
English	90.70	89.92	$8 \cdot 10^{-5}$
German	91.64	91.25	0.0574
Greek	84.34	82.84	0.0000
Hungarian	82.72	81.87	$2 \cdot 10^{-3}$
Italian	87.30	84.53	0.0000
Japanese	93.80	93.64	0.5144
Portuguese	90.65	88.81	0.0000
Slovene	83.47	80.84	0.0000
Spanish	83.98	80.90	0.0000
Swedish	89.85	88.49	$4 \cdot 10^{-5}$
Turkish	86.77	87.10	0.9383

where MIMICK outperforms Char→Tag. This analysis demonstrates that when the performance gap between two algorithms becomes narrower, inquiring for more information (i.e., identifying the domains with effect rather than just estimating their number), may result in weaker results. For completeness, we also performed the analysis for the independent dataset setups with $\alpha = 0.01$. The results are $(\hat{k}_{count}, \hat{k}_{Bonferroni}, \hat{k}_{Fisher})$: Mate vs. SpaCy: (7,7,7); Mate vs. Redshift (1,0,2); MIMICK vs. Char→Tag: (7,5,13).

Dependent Datasets   In cross-domain sentiment classification (Table 6.4) and word similarity prediction (Table 6.6), the involved datasets manifest mutual dependence. Particularly, each sentiment setup shares its test dataset with two other setups, while in word similarity WS-353 is the union of WS-353-REL and WS-353-SIM. As discussed in Section 6.4, $\hat{k}_{Bonferroni}$ is the appropriate estimator of the number of cases one algorithm outperforms another.

Table 6.6: Spearman's ρ values for the best performing predict model (W2V-CBOW) of Baroni et al. [2014] and the GLOVE model. $*$ and $+$ are as in Table 6.4.

Dataset	W2V	GLOVE	ρ-Value
WS353*,+	0.73	0.62	$2 \cdot 10^{-5}$
WS353-SIM*,+	0.78	0.69	0.0000
WS353-REL	0.68	0.57	0.2123
MC-30*,+	0.82	0.77	$1 \cdot 10^{-3}$
RG-65	0.83	0.81	0.3053
RW	0.48	0.41	0.2426
MEN*	0.79	0.73	0.0021
MTurk-287	0.67	0.64	0.2076
MTurk-771	0.71	0.68	0.0425
YP-130*,+	0.50	0.53	0.0000
SimLex999*	0.46	0.37	0.0015
$Verb - 143$	0.44	0.32	0.0431

The results in Table 6.1 manifest the phenomenon demonstrated by the second toy example in Section 6.6, which shows that when the datasets are dependent, $\hat{k}_{Fisher}$ as well as the error-prone $\hat{k}_{count}$ may be too optimistic regarding the number of datasets with effect. This stands in contrast to $\hat{k}_{Bonferroni}$ which controls the probability to overestimate the number of such datasets.

Indeed, $\hat{k}_{Bonferroni}$ is much more conservative, yielding values of 6 ($\alpha = 0.05$) and 2 ($\alpha = 0.01$) for sentiment, and of 6 ($\alpha = 0.05$) and 4 ($\alpha = 0.01$) for word similarity. The differences from the conclusions that might have been drawn by $\hat{k}_{count}$ are again quite substantial. The difference between $\hat{k}_{Bonferroni}$ and $\hat{k}_{count}$ in sentiment classification is 4, which accounts to 1/3 of the 12 test setups. Even for word similarity, the difference between the two methods, which account to 2 for both α values, represents 1/6 of the 12 test setups. The domains identified by the Holm procedure are marked in the tables.

6.7.4   RESULTS SUMMARY AND OVERVIEW

Our goal in this section was to compare two approaches. In the current counting practice one reports the number of datasets for which the difference between the algorithms reaches a pre-defined significance level. This approach is denoted here with $\hat{k}_{count}$ and shown to be statistically not valid in Sections 6.6 and 6.7. In contrast, in the replicability analysis framework we advocate here the computation is more complicated but it comes with statistical guarantees.

We observe that the two approaches yield quite different results. This happens especially in evaluation setups where the differences between the algorithms are small for most datasets. In some cases, when the datasets are independent, our analysis has the power to declare a larger number of datasets with effect than the number of individual significant test values ($\hat{k}_{count}$). In other cases, when the datasets are interdependent, $\hat{k}_{count}$ is too optimistic.

Our proposed analysis changes the observations that might have been made based on the papers where the results analyzed here were originally reported. For example, for the Mate-Redshift comparison (independent evaluation sets), we show that there is evidence that the number of datasets with effect is much higher than one would assume based on counting the significant sets (5 vs. 2 out of 7 evaluation sets), giving a stronger claim regarding the superiority of Mate. In multilingual POS tagging (again, a setup of independent evaluation sets) our analysis shows evidence for 16 sets with effect compared to only 11 of the erroneous count method, a difference in 5 out of 23 evaluation sets (21.7%). Finally, in the cross-domain sentiment classification and the word similarity judgment tasks (dependent evaluation sets), the unjustified counting method may be too optimistic (e.g., 10 vs. 6 out of 12 evaluation sets, for $\alpha = 0.05$ in the sentiment task), in favor of the new algorithms.

CHAPTER 7

Open Questions and Challenges

In this chapter we would like to point on several issues that remain open even after our investigation. We hope that bringing these issues to the attention of the research community will encourage our fellow researchers to come up with appropriate solutions.

The first open issue is that of *dependent observations*. An assumption shared by the statistical significance tests discussed in this book is that the data samples are independent and identically distributed. This assumption, however, is rarely true in NLP setups. For example, the popular WSJ Penn Treebank corpus [Marcus et al., 1993] consists of 2,499 articles from a three year Wall Street Journal (WSJ) collection of 98,732 stories. Obviously, some of the sentences included in the corpus come from the same article, were written by the same author or were reviewed before publication by the same editor. As another example, many sentences in the Europarl parallel corpus [Koehn, 2005], which is very popular in the machine translation literature, are taken from the same parliament discussion. An independence assumption between the sentences in these corpora is not likely to hold.

This dependence between test examples violates the conditions under which the theoretical guarantees of most significance tests were developed. The impact of this phenomenon on our results is hard to quantify, partly because it is hard to quantify the nature of the dependence between test set examples in NLP datasets. Some papers are even discussing the possibility of abandoning the statistical significance testing framework (Chapters 2 and 3) due to this hard-to-meet assumption [Carver, 1978, Koplenig, 2017, Leek et al., 2017, McShane et al., 2017]. In our opinion, this calls for a future collaboration with statisticians in order to better understand the extent to which existing popular significance tests are relevant for NLP, and to develop alternative tests when necessary.

Another issue that deserves some more thinking is that of *cross-validation*. To increase the validity of reported results, it is customary in NLP papers to generate multiple random splits of the experimental corpus into train, development and test portions. For each such split (fold), the tested algorithms are trained and tuned on the training and development datasets, respectively, and their results on the test data are recorded. The final reported result is typically the average of the test set results across the splits, and some papers also report the fraction of the folds for which one algorithm performs better than the others. While cross-validation is surely a desired practice, it is challenging to report statistical significance when it is employed. Particularly, the test sets of the different folds are obviously not independent, their content is even likely to overlap.

One solution we would like to propose here is based on replicability analysis (Chapter 6), which proposes a statistical significance framework for multiple comparisons performed with dependent test sets, using the $K_{Bonferroni}$ estimator for the number of datasets with significant effect. One statistically sound way to test for significance when a cross-validation protocol is employed is hence to calculate the p-value for each fold separately, and then to perform replicability analysis for dependent datasets with $K_{Bonferroni}$. Only if this analysis rejects the null hypothesis in all folds (or in more than a predefined threshold number of folds), the results should be declared significant. Here again further statistical investigation may lead to additional, potentially better, solutions.

Another issue has to do with the *statistical power of replicability analysis*. The framework we propose addresses two different situations encountered in NLP: independent and dependent datasets. For dependent datasets, we assumed that the type of dependency cannot be determined. One could use more powerful methods if certain assumptions on the dependency between the test statistics could be made. For example, one could use the partial conjunction p-value based on the Simes test for the global null hypothesis [Simes, 1986], which was proposed by Benjamini and Heller [2008] for the case where the test statistics satisfy certain positive dependency properties (see Theorem 1 in Benjamini and Heller [2008]). Using this partial conjunction p-value rather than the one based on Bonferroni, one may obtain higher values of $\hat{k}$ with the same statistical guarantee. Similarly, for the identification question, if certain positive dependency properties hold, Holm's procedure could be replaced by Hochberg's or Hommel's procedures [Hochberg, 1988, Hommel, 1988] which are more powerful. An alternative, more powerful multiple testing procedure for identification of datasets with effect, is the method described in Benjamini and Hochberg [1995], that controls the false discovery rate (FDR). This is a less strict error criterion than the one considered by our replicability framework. This method is more appropriate in cases where one may tolerate some errors as long as the proportion of errors among all the claims made is small, as expected to happen when the number of datasets grows.

A question that naturally raises is when a multiple comparison framework should be employed. We note that the increase in the number of evaluation datasets may have positive and negative aspects. On the one hand, we believe that multiple comparisons are integral to NLP research when aiming to develop algorithms that perform well across languages and domains. On the other hand, experimenting with multiple evaluation sets that reflect very similar linguistic phenomena may only complicate the comparison between alternative algorithms. In fact, our replicability framework is useful mostly where the datasets are heterogeneous, coming from different languages or domains. When they are just technically different but could potentially be just combined into a one big dataset, then we believe the question of Demšar [2006], whether at least one dataset shows evidence for effect, is more appropriate.

Finally, a natural question that we did not address in this book is the statistically sound analysis of multiple comparisons (Chapter 6) where the compared model are non-deterministic (Chapter 5). We believe that some feedback on the application of the ideas discussed in this book is required so that a proper framework for such cases can be developed. We hence leave this investigation for future research.

CHAPTER 8

Conclusions

This book has addressed the application of statistical significance testing to NLP research. The perspective we took is that of a comparison between two algorithms based on their performance on one or several datasets, which is the common evaluation setup in experimental NLP papers.

Our focus has been on three problems. We first addressed the fundamental problem of proper application of significance tests when two deterministic algorithms are compared based on their performance on a single dataset. Next, we extended this framework to the comparison between non-deterministic algorithms such as DNNs and to the comparison between two algorithms across many datasets. We augmented our presentation with a list of open problems and a discussion of the limitations of our framework.

Our main goal has been to provide clear guidelines to NLP researchers who would like to be statistically rigorous but lack the theoretical foundations. Chapters 4–6 are designed to serve as a handbook and contain detailed recommendations of statistical tests and procedures to be employed in specific common cases. Particularly, Chapter 4 provides a list of NLP tasks and evaluation measures, and matches each task and measure with appropriate statistical significance tests. In addition, we provide a decision tree that guides the choice between parametric and non-parametric tests in each of the cases (Figure 4.3). Chapter 5 discusses the comparison between two deep neural models that are sensitive to hyper-parameter selection, and Algorithm 5.12 provides an explicit procedure of how to perform such comparisons. Finally, Chapter 6 is concerned with proper analysis of multiple comparisons. Its summary provides guidelines about the measures to be computed in order to solve the counting and identification problems, both when the comparisons are independent and when such an independence assumption cannot be made.

We hope this monograph will highlight the importance of statistical significance testing in particular and theoretically sound evaluation in general to NLP research. As long as experimental analysis is the core method of determining the quality of NLP algorithms, the importance of such evaluation cannot be overstated.

Bibliography

Agirre, Eneko, Alfonseca, Enrique, Hall, Keith, Kravalova, Jana, Paşca, Marius, and Soroa, Aitor, A study on similarity and relatedness using distributional and wordnet-based approaches, *Proc. of the North American Chapter of the Association for Computational Linguistics*, 2009. DOI: 10.3115/1620754.1620758. 66

Álvarez-Esteban, P. C., del Barrio, Eustasio, Cuesta-Albertos, Juan Antonio, and Matrán, C., Models for the assessment of treatment improvement: The ideal and the feasible, *Statistical Science*, 32(3):469–485, 2017. DOI: 10.1214/17-sts616.

Al-Rfou, Rami, Perozzi, Bryan, and Skiena, Steven, Polyglot: Distributed word representations for multilingual NLP, *Proc. of the Special Interest Group on Natural Language Learning Conference on Computational Natural Language Learning*, 2013. 65

Anderson, Theodore W. and Darling, Donald A., A test of goodness of fit, *Journal of the American Statistical Association*, 49(268):765–769, 2005. DOI: 10.1080/01621459.1954.10501232. 11

Bagga, Amit and Baldwin, Breck, Algorithms for scoring coreference chains, *The 1st International Conference on Language Resources and Evaluation Workshop on Linguistics Conference*, 1:563–566, 1998.

Baker, Simon, Reichart, Roi, and Korhonen, Anna, An unsupervised model for instance level subcategorization acquisition, *Proc. of the Conference on Empirical Methods in Natural Language Processing*, 2014. DOI: 10.3115/v1/d14-1034. 66

Banarescu, Laura, Bonial, Claire, Cai, Shu, Georgescu, Madalina, Griffitt, Kira, Hermjakob, Ulf, Knight, Kevin, Koehn, Philipp, Palmer, Martha, and Schneider, Nathan, Abstract meaning representation for sembanking, *Proc. of the 7th Linguistic Annotation Workshop and Interoperability with Discourse*, pages 178–186, 2013. 26

Banerjee, Satanjeev and Lavie, Alon, METEOR: An automatic metric for MT evaluation with improved correlation with human judgments, *Proc. of the Association for Computational Linguistics Workshop on Intrinsic and Extrinsic Evaluation Measures for Machine Translation and/or Summarization*, 2005. 27, 31

Baroni, Marco, Dinu, Georgiana, and Kruszewski, Germán, Don't count, predict! A systematic comparison of context-counting vs. context-predicting semantic vectors, *Proc. of the Association for Computational Linguistics*, 2014. DOI: 10.3115/v1/p14-1023. 54, 66, 72

Barzilay, Regina and Kan, Min-Yen, *Proc. of the 55th Annual Meeting of the Association for Computational Linguistics (Volume 1:Long Papers)*, *Proc. of the Association for Computational Linguistics*, 2017. DOI: 10.18653/v1/p17-1.

Blitzer, John, Dredze, Mark, and Pereira, Fernando, Biographies, Bollywood, boom-boxes and blenders: Domain adaptation for sentiment classification, *Proc. of the Association for Computational Linguistics*, 2007. 54, 66

Blitzer, John, McDonald, Ryan, and Pereira, Fernando, Domain adaptation with structural correspondence learning, *Proc. of the Conference on Empirical Methods in Natural Language Processing*, 2006. DOI: 10.3115/1610075.1610094. 18, 54

Bonferroni, Carlo E., Teoria statistica delle classi e calcolo delle probabilita, *Libreria Internazionale Seeber*, 1936. DOI: 10.4135/9781412961288.n455.

Bretz, Frank, Hothorn, Torsten, and Westfall, Peter, *Multiple Comparisons Using R*, Chapman and Hall/CRC, 2016. DOI: 10.1201/9781420010909. xv

Bruni, Elia, Boleda, Gemma, Baroni, Marco, and Tran, Nam-Khanh, Distributional semantics in technicolor, *Proc. of the Association for Computational Linguistics*, 2012. 66

Buchholz, Sabine and Marsi, Erwin, CoNLL-X shared task on multilingual dependency parsing, *Proc. of the Special Interest Group on Natural Language Learning Conference on Computational Natural Language Learning*, 2006. DOI: 10.3115/1596276.1596305. 52, 65

Bohnet, Bernd, Very high accuracy and fast dependency parsing is not a contradiction, *Proc. of the International Conference on Computational Linguistics*, 2010. 65

Bontcheva, Kalina, Roberts, Ian, Derczynski, Leon, and Rout, Dominic Paul, The GATE crowdsourcing plugin: Crowdsourcing annotated corpora made easy, *Proc. of the European Chapter of the Association for Computational Linguistics*, 2014. DOI: 10.3115/v1/e14-2025.

Bruni, Elia, Tran, Nam-Khanh, and Baroni, Marco, Multimodal distributional semantics, *Journal of Artificial Intelligence Research*, 49:1–47, 2014. DOI: 10.1613/jair.4135. 54

Begley, C. Glenn and Ellis, Lee M., Drug development: Raise standards for preclinical cancer research, *Nature*, 483(7391):531–533, 2012. DOI: 10.1038/483531a. 51

Berger, Roger L., A nonparametric, intersection-union test for stochastic order, *Statistical Decision Theory and Related Topics, IV*, 2:253–264, 1988. DOI: 10.1007/978-1-4612-3818-8_20.

Berg-Kirkpatrick, Taylor, Burkett, David, and Klein, Dan, An empirical investigation of statistical significance in NLP, *Proc. of the Joint Conference on Empirical Methods in Natural Language Processing and Computational Natural Language Learning*, 2012. 14, 55, 66

Benjamini, Yoav and Hochberg, Yosef, Controlling the false discovery rate: A practical and powerful approach to multiple testing, *Journal of the Royal Statistical Society. Series B (Methodological)*, pages 289–300, 1995. DOI: 10.1111/j.2517-6161.1995.tb02031.x. 76

Benjamini, Yoav, Krieger, Abba M., and Yekutieli, Daniel, Adaptive linear step-up procedures that control the false discovery rate, *Biometrika*, pages 491–507, 2006. DOI: 10.1093/biomet/93.3.491. 64

Benjamini, Yoav and Heller, Ruth, Screening for partial conjunction hypotheses, *Biometrics*, 64(4):1215–1222, 2008. DOI: 10.1111/j.1541-0420.2007.00984.x. 53, 57, 58, 60, 76

Benjamini, Yoav, Heller, Ruth, and Yekutieli, Daniel, Selective inference in complex research, *Philosophical Transactions of the Royal Society of London A: Mathematical, Physical and Engineering Sciences*, 367(1906):4255–4271, 2009. DOI: 10.1098/rsta.2009.0127. 53, 58

Benjamini, Yoav and Bogomolov, Marina, Selective inference on multiple families of hypotheses, *Journal of the Royal Statistical Society: Series B (Statistical Methodology)*, 76(1):297–318, 2014. DOI: 10.1111/rssb.12028.

Carver, Ronald, The case against statistical significance testing, *Harvard Educational Review*, 48(3):378–399, 1978. DOI: 10.17763/haer.48.3.t490261645281841. 75

Chan, Yee Seng and Ng, Hwee Tou, Domain adaptation with active learning for word sense disambiguation, *Proc. of the Association for Computational Linguistics*, 2007. 54

Chan, Yee Seng, Ng, Hwee Tou, and Chiang, David, Word sense disambiguation improves statistical machine translation, *Proc. of the Association for Computational Linguistics*, 2007. 18

Charniak, Eugene, A maximum-entropy-inspired parser, *Proc. of the North American Chapter of the Association for Computational Linguistics*, 2000. 52

Chen, David L. and Dolan, William B., Collecting highly parallel data for paraphrase evaluation, *Proc. of the 49th Annual Meeting of the Association for Computational Linguistics: Human Language Technologies*, 1:190–200, 2011. 4, 31

Chen, Minmin, Chen, Yixin, and Weinberger, Kilian Q., Automatic feature decomposition for single view co-training, *Proc. of the International Conference on Machine Learning*, 2011. 66

Papineni, Kishore, Learning phrase representations using RNN encoder-decoder for statistical machine translation, *Proc. of the Conference on Empirical Methods in Natural Language Processing*, pages 1724–1734, 2014. DOI: 10.3115/v1/D14-1179. 3

Choi, Jinho D., Tetreault, Joel, and Stent, Amanda, It depends: Dependency parser comparison using a web-based evaluation tool, *Proc. of the Association for Computational Linguistics*, 2015. DOI: 10.3115/v1/p15-1038. 65

Clark, Jonathan H., Dyer, Chris, Lavie, Alon, and Smith, Noah A., Better hypothesis testing for statistical machine translation: Controlling for optimizer instability, *Proc. of the 49th Annual Meeting of the Association for Computational Linguistics: Human Language Technologies*, pages 176–181, 2015. 35, 38

Cochran, William G., The comparison of percentages in matched samples, *Biometrika*, 37(3/4):256–266, 1950. DOI: 10.2307/2332378. 18

Cohen, Jacob, A coefficient of agreement for nominal scales, *Educational and Psychological Measurement*, 20(1):37–46, 1960. DOI: 10.1177/001316446002000104.

Cohen, Paul R., *Empirical Methods for Artificial Intelligence*, MIT Press, Cambridge, MA, 139, 1995. 21

Collins, Michael, Head-driven statistical models for natural language parsing, *Computational Linguistics*, 29(4):589–637, 2003. DOI: 10.1162/089120103322753356. 52

Collins, Michael, Koehn, Philipp, and Kucerova, Ivona, Clause restructuring for statistical machine translation, *Proc. of the Association for Computational Linguistics*, 2005. DOI: 10.3115/1219840.1219906. 18

Daumé III, Hal, Frustratingly easy domain adaptation, *Proc. of the Association for Computational Linguistics*, 2007. 54

Dauphin, Yann N., Pascanu, Razvan, Gulcehre, Caglar, Cho, Kyunghyun, Ganguli, Surya, and Bengio, Yoshua, Identifying and attacking the saddle point problem in high-dimensional non-convex optimization, *Advances in Neural Information Processing Systems*, pages 2933–2941, 2014. 35

del Barrio, Eustasio, Cuesta-Albertos, Juan A., and Matrán, Carlos, An optimal transportation approach for assessing almost stochastic order, *The Mathematics of the Uncertain*, pages 33–44, 2018. DOI: 10.1007/978-3-319-73848-2_3. 42, 43, 44

De Marneffe, Marie-Catherine, Dozat, Timothy, Silveira, Natalia, Haverinen, Katri, Ginter, Filip, Nivre, Joakim, and Manning, Christopher D., Stanford dependencies: A cross-linguistic typology, *Proc. of the International Conference on Language Resources and Evaluation*, 2014. 65

Demšar, Janez, Statistical comparisons of classifiers over multiple data sets, *Journal of Machine Learning Research*, 7:1–30, 2006. 54, 55, 76

Dietterich, Thomas G., Approximate statistical tests for comparing supervised classification learning algorithms, *Neural Computation*, 10(7):1895–1923, 1998. DOI: 10.1162/089976698300017197. 54

Dozat, Timothy and Manning, Christopher D., Deep biaffine attention for neural dependency parsing, *Proc. of the International Conference on Learning Representations*, 2017. 35

Dror, Rotem, Baumer, Gili, Bogomolov, Marina, and Reichart, Roi, Replicability analysis for natural language processing: Testing significance with multiple datasets, *Transactions of the Association for Computational Linguistics*, 5:471–486, 2017. DOI: 10.1162/tacl_a_00074. xiv, xv, 2

Dror, Rotem, Baumer, Gili, Shlomov, Segev, and Reichart, Roi, The hitchhiker's guide to testing statistical significance in natural language processing, *Proc. of the 56th Annual Meeting of the Association for Computational Linguistics*, 1:1383–1392, 2018. DOI: 10.18653/v1/p18-1128. xiii, xv, 1

Dror, Rotem, Shlomov, Segev, and Reichart, Roi, Deep dominance-how to properly compare deep neural models, *Proc. of the 57th Conference of the Association for Computational Linguistics*, pages 2773–2785, 2019. DOI: 10.18653/v1/p19-1266. xiv, xv, 2, 36

Dunn, Olive Jean, Multiple comparisons among means, *Journal of the American Statistical Association*, 56(293):52–64, 1961. DOI: 10.1080/01621459.1961.10482090.

Efron, Bradley and Tibshirani, Robert J., *An Introduction to the Bootstrap*, CRC Press, 1994. DOI: 10.1007/978-1-4899-4541-9. 19, 20, 21, 66

El Barmi, Hammou and McKeague, Ian W., Empirical likelihood-based tests for stochastic ordering, *Bernoulli: Official Journal of the Bernoulli Society for Mathematical Statistics and Probability*, 19(1):295, 2013. DOI: 10.3150/11-bej393. 41

Farcomeni, Alessio, A review of modern multiple hypothesis testing, with particular attention to the false discovery proportion, *Statistical Methods in Medical Research*, 2007. DOI: 10.1177/0962280206079046. 57

Faruqui, Manaal and Dyer, Chris, Community evaluation and exchange of word vectors at `wordvectors.org`, *Proc. of the Association for Computational Linguistics: System Demonstrations*, 2014. DOI: 10.3115/v1/p14-5004. 66

Faruqui, Manaal, Tsvetkov, Yulia, Rastogi, Pushpendre, and Dyer, Chris, Problems with evaluation of word embeddings using word similarity tasks, *ArXiv Preprint ArXiv:1605.02276*, 2016. DOI: 10.18653/v1/w16-2506.

Finkel, Jenny Rose, Kleeman, Alex, and Manning, Christopher D., Efficient, feature-based, conditional random field parsing, *Proc. of the Association for Computational Linguistics: Human Language Technologies*, pages 959–967, 2008. 35

Finkelstein, Lev, Gabrilovich, Evgeniy, Matias, Yossi, Rivlin, Ehud, Solan, Zach, Wolfman, Gadi, and Ruppin, Eytan, Placing search in context: The concept revisited, *Proc. of the International World Wide Web Conference*, 2001. DOI: 10.1145/371920.372094. 54, 66

Fisher, Ronald Aylmer, *The Design of Experiments*, Oliver and Boyd, Edinburgh, London, 1937. 13

Gibbons, Jean Dickinson and Chakraborti, Subhabrata, Nonparametric statistical inference, *International Encyclopedia of Statistical Science*, pages 977–979, 2011. DOI: 10.1007/978-3-642-04898-2_420. 17

Glorot, Xavier and Bengio, Yoshua, Understanding the difficulty of training deep feedforward neural networks, *Proc. of the 13th International Conference on Artificial Intelligence and Statistics*, pages 249–256, 2010. 36

Graves, Alex, Generating sequences with recurrent neural networks, *ArXiv Preprint ArXiv:1308.0850*, 2013. 23

Guo, Honglei, Zhu, Huijia, Guo, Zhili, Zhang, Xiaoxun, Wu, Xian, and Su, Zhong, Domain adaptation with latent semantic association for named entity recognition, *Proc. of the North American Chapter of the Association for Computational Linguistics*, 2009. DOI: 10.3115/1620754.1620795. 54

Halawi, Guy, Dror, Gideon, Gabrilovich, Evgeniy, and Koren, Yehuda, Large-scale learning of word relatedness with constraints, *Proc. of Association for Computing Machinery Special Interest Group on Knowledge Discovery in Data*, 2012. DOI: 10.1145/2339530.2339751. 66

Heller, Ruth, Bogomolov, Marina, and Benjamini, Yoav, Deciding whether follow-up studies have replicated findings in a preliminary large-scale omics study, *Proc. of the National Academy of Sciences*, 111(46):16262–16267, 2014. DOI: 10.1073/pnas.1314814111. xiv, 2, 51, 52

Heller, Ruth and Yekutieli, Daniel, Replicability analysis for genome-wide association studies, *The Annals of Applied Statistics*, 8(1):481–498, 2014. DOI: 10.1214/13-aoas697.

Hershcovich, Daniel, Abend, Omri, and Rappoport, Ari, A transition-based directed acyclic graph parser for UCCA, *Proc. of the 55th Annual Meeting of the Association for Computational Linguistics*, 1:1127–1138, 2017. DOI: 10.18653/v1/p17-1104. 35

Herndon, Thomas, Ash, Michael, and Pollin, Robert, Does high public debt consistently stifle economic growth? A critique of Reinhart and Rogoff, *Cambridge Journal of Economics*, 38(2):257–279, 2014. DOI: 10.1093/cje/bet075. 51

Hill, Felix, Reichart, Roi, and Korhonen, Anna, Simlex-999: Evaluating semantic models with (genuine) similarity estimation, *Computational Linguistics*, 41(4):665–695, 2015. DOI: 10.1162/coli_a_00237. 54, 66

Hinton, Geoffrey, Srivastava, Nitish, and Swersky, Kevin, Neural networks for machine learning lecture 6a overview of mini-batch gradient descent, *Lecture 6a*, 2012. 46

Hochberg, Yosef, A sharper Bonferroni procedure for multiple tests of significance, *Biometrika*, 75(4):800–802, 1988. DOI: 10.1093/biomet/75.4.800. 76

Hochreiter, Sepp and Schmidhuber, Jürgen, Long short-term memory, *Neural Computation*, 9(8):1735–1780, 1997. DOI: 10.1162/neco.1997.9.8.1735. 35

Hofmann, Marko A., Searching for effects in big data: Why p-values are not advised and what to use instead, *Winter Simulation Conference*, pages 725–736, 2015. DOI: 10.1109/wsc.2015.7408210. 33

Holm, Sture, A simple sequentially rejective multiple test procedure, *Scandinavian Journal of Statistics*, 6(2):65–70, 1979. 61

Hommel, Gerhard, A stagewise rejective multiple test procedure based on a modified Bonferroni test, *Biometrika*, 75(2):383–386, 1988. DOI: 10.1093/biomet/75.2.383. 76

Honnibal, Matthew, Goldberg, Yoav, and Johnson, Mark, A non-monotonic arc-eager transition system for dependency parsing, *Proc. of the Special Interest Group on Natural Language Learning Conference on Computational Natural Language Learning*, 2013. 65

Honnibal, Matthew and Johnson, Mark, An improved non-monotonic transition system for dependency parsing, *Proc. of the Conference on Empirical Methods in Natural Language Processing*, 2015. DOI: 10.18653/v1/d15-1162. 65

Johnson, Richard A. and Bhattacharyya, Gouri K., *Statistics: Principles and Methods*, John Wiley & Sons, 2019. xv

Kasuya, Eiiti, Mann-Whitney U test when variances are unequal, *Animal Behaviour*, 6(61):1247–1249, 2001. DOI: 10.1006/anbe.2001.1691.

Kingma, Diederik P. and Ba, Jimmy, Adam: A method for stochastic optimization, *ArXiv Preprint ArXiv:1412.6980*, 2014. 46

Kiperwasser, Eliyahu and Goldberg, Yoav, Simple and accurate dependency parsing using bidirectional LSTM feature representations, *Transactions of the Association for Computational Linguistics*, 4:313–327, 2016. DOI: 10.1162/tacl_a_00101. 10

Koehn, Philipp, Statistical significance tests for machine translation evaluation, *Proc. of the Conference on Empirical Methods in Natural Language Processing*, 2004. 21

Koehn, Philipp, Europarl: A parallel corpus for statistical machine translation, *Proc. of the Machine Translation Summit*, 2005. 10, 54, 75

Koehn, Philipp, Hoang, Hieu, Birch, Alexandra, Callison-Burch, Chris, Federico, Marcello, Bertoldi, Nicola, Cowan, Brooke, Shen, Wade, Moran, Christine, Zens, Richard, Dyer, Chris, Bojar, Ondrej, Constantin, Alexandra, and Herbst, Evan, Moses: Open source toolkit for statistical machine translation, *Proc. of the 45th Annual Meeting of the Association for Computational Linguistics Companion Volume Proceedings of the Demo and Poster Sessions*, pages 177–180, 2007. DOI: 10.3115/1557769.1557821. 3

Koehn, Philipp and Schroeder, Josh, Experiments in domain adaptation for statistical machine translation, *Proc. of the 2nd Workshop on Statistical Machine Translation*, 2007. DOI: 10.3115/1626355.1626388. 54

Koplenig, Alexander, Against statistical significance testing in corpus linguistics, *Corpus Linguistics and Linguistic Theory*, 2017. DOI: 10.1515/cllt-2016-0036. 75

Krippendorff, Klaus, Computing Krippendorff's alpha-reliability, *Departmental Papers (ASC)*, 2011.

Kübler, Sandra, McDonald, Ryan, and Nivre, Joakim, Dependency parsing, *Synthesis Lectures on Human Language Technologies*, 1(1):1–127, 2009. DOI: 10.2200/s00169ed1v01y200901hlt002. 31

Lample, Guillaume, Ballesteros, Miguel, Subramanian, Sandeep, Kawakami, Kazuya, and Dyer, Chris, Neural architectures for named entity recognition, *ArXiv Preprint ArXiv:1603.01360*, 2016. DOI: 10.18653/v1/n16-1030. 45, 46

Lee, Young Jack and Wolfe, Douglas A., A distribution-free test for stochastic ordering, *Journal of the American Statistical Association*, 71(355):722–727, 1976. DOI: 10.1080/01621459.1976.10481555. 41

Lee, Heeyoung, Recasens, Marta, Chang, Angel, Surdeanu, Mihai, and Jurafsky, Dan, Joint entity and event coreference resolution across documents, *Proc. of the Joint Conference on Empirical Methods in Natural Language Processing and Computational Natural Language Learning*, pages 489–500, 2012.

Lee, Ihno A. and Preacher, Kristopher J., Calculation for the test of the difference between two dependent correlations with one variable in common, *[Computer Software]*, 2013.

Lehmann, Erich Leo, Ordered families of distributions, *The Annals of Mathematical Statistics*, pages 399–419, 1955. DOI: 10.1214/aoms/1177728487. 39

Leek, Jeffrey T. and Peng, Roger D., Opinion: Reproducible research can still be wrong: Adopting a prevention approach, *Proc. of the National Academy of Sciences*, 112(6):1645–1646, 2015. DOI: 10.1073/pnas.1421412111. 52

Leek, Jeff, McShane, Blakeley B., Gelman, Andrew, Colquhoun, David, Nuijten, Michèle B., and Goodman, Steven N., Five ways to fix statistics, *Nature*, 551(7682):557–559, 2017. DOI: 10.1038/d41586-017-07522-z. 75

Leviant, Ira and Reichart, Roi, Separated by an un-common language: Towards judgment language informed vector space modeling, *ArXiv Preprint ArXiv:1508.00106*, 2015. 14

Levy, Omer and Goldberg, Yoav, Dependency-based word embeddings, *Proc. of the Association for Computational Linguistics*, 2014. DOI: 10.3115/v1/p14-2050. 54

Li, Junhui, Xiong, Deyi, Tu, Zhaopeng, Zhu, Muhua, Zhang, Min, and Zhou, Guodong, Modeling source syntax for neural machine translation, *Proc. of the Association for Computational Linguistics*, 2017. DOI: 10.18653/v1/p17-1064. 21

Liang, Percy, Lambda dependency-based compositional semantics, *ArXiv Preprint ArXiv:1309.4408*, 2013. 26

Lin, Chin-Yew, Rouge: A package for automatic evaluation of summaries, *Text Summarization Branches Out: Proceedings of the Association for Computational Linguistics Workshop*, 2004. 31

Ling, Wang, Dyer, Chris, Black, Alan W., Trancoso, Isabel, Fermandez, Ramon, Amir, Silvio, Marujo, Luis, and Luis, Tiago, Finding function in form: Compositional character models for open vocabulary word representation, *Proc. of the Conference on Empirical Methods in Natural Language Processing*, 2015. DOI: 10.18653/v1/d15-1176. 65

Loughin, Thomas M., A systematic comparison of methods for combining p-values from independent tests, *Computational Statistics and Data Analysis*, 47(3):467–485, 2004. DOI: 10.1016/j.csda.2003.11.020. 58

Luo, Xiaoqiang, On coreference resolution performance metrics, *Proc. of the Conference on Human Language Technology and Empirical Methods in Natural Language Processing*, pages 25–32, 2005. DOI: 10.3115/1220575.1220579.

Luong, Minh-Thang, Socher, Richard, and Manning, Christopher D., Better word representations with recursive neural networks for morphology, *Proc. of the Special Interest Group on Natural Language Learning Conference on Computational Natural Language Learning*, 2013. 66

Ma, Xuezhe and Hovy, Eduard, End-to-end sequence labeling via bi-directional LSTM-CNNs-CRF, *ArXiv Preprint ArXiv:1603.01354*, 2016. DOI: 10.18653/v1/p16-1101. 45, 46

Mann, Henry B. and Whitney, Donald R., On a test of whether one of two random variables is stochastically larger than the other, *The Annals of Mathematical Statistics*, pages 50–60, 1947. DOI: 10.1214/aoms/1177730491. 39

Marcus, Mitchell P., Marcinkiewicz, Mary Ann, and Santorini, Beatrice, Building a large annotated corpus of English: The Penn treebank, *Computational Linguistics*, 19(2):313–330, 1993. DOI: 10.21236/ada273556. 10, 45, 52, 75

Marrese-Taylor, Edison and Matsuo, Yutaka, Replication issues in syntax-based aspect extraction for opinion mining, *Proc. of the Student Research Workshop at the European Chapter of the Association for Computational Linguistics*, 2017. DOI: 10.18653/v1/e17-4003. 52

Martins, André F. T., Smith, Noah A., Xing, Eric P., Aguiar, Pedro M. Q., and Figueiredo, Mário A. T., Turbo parsers: Dependency parsing by approximate variational inference, *Proc. of the Conference on Empirical Methods in Natural Language Processing*, 2010. 65

Martins, Andre, Almeida, Miguel, and Smith, Noah A., Turning on the turbo: Fast third-order non-projective turbo parsers, *Proc. of the 51st Annual Meeting of the Association for Computational Linguistics*, 2:617–622, 2013. 10

Massey Jr., Frank J., The Kolmogorov-Smirnov test for goodness of fit, *Journal of the American Statistical Association*, 46(253):68–78, 1951. DOI: 10.1080/01621459.1951.10500769.

McShane, Blakeley B., Gal, David, Gelman, Andrew, Robert, Christian, and Tackett, Jennifer L., Abandon statistical significance, *ArXiv Preprint ArXiv:1709.07588*, 2017. DOI: 10.1080/00031305.2018.1527253. 75

McNemar, Quinn, Note on the sampling error of the difference between correlated proportions or percentages, *Psychometrika*, 12(2):153–157, 1947. DOI: 10.1007/bf02295996. 18, 67

Mikolov, Tomas, Sutskever, Ilya, Chen, Kai, Corrado, Gregory S., and Dean, Jeffrey, Distributed representations of Words and phrases and their compositionality, *Proc. of the Neural Information Processing Systems*, 2013. 54, 66

Miller, George A. and Charles, Walter G., Contextual correlates of semantic similarity, *Language and Cognitive Processes*, 6(1):1–28, 1991. DOI: 10.1080/01690969108406936. 66

Montgomery, Douglas C. and Runger, George C., *Applied Statistics and Probability for Engineers*, John Wiley & Sons, 2007. xv

Moonesinghe, Ramal, Khoury, Muin J., and Janssens, A. Cecile J. W., Most published research findings are false but a little replication goes a long way, *PLoS Med*, 4(2):e28, 2007. DOI: 10.1371/journal.pmed.0040028. 51

Murdoch, Duncan J., Tsai, Yu-Ling, and Adcock, James, P-values are random variables, *The American Statistician*, 62(3):242–245, 2008. DOI: 10.1198/000313008x332421.

Névéol, Aurélie, Grouin, Cyril, Cohen, Kevin Bretonnel, and Robert, Aude, Replicability of research in biomedical natural language processing: A pilot evaluation for a coding task, *Proc. of the Conference on Empirical Methods in Natural Language Processing*, 2016. DOI: 10.18653/v1/w16-6110. 52

Nilsson, Jens, Riedel, Sebastian, and Yuret, Deniz, The CoNLL 2007 shared task on dependency parsing, *Proc. of the Special Interest Group on Natural Language Learning Conference on Computational Natural Language Learning*, 2007. 52, 65

Nivre, Joakim, Hall, Johan, Kübler, Sandra, McDonald, Ryan, Nilsson, Jens, Riedel, Sebastian, and Yuret, Deniz, The CoNLL 2007 shared task on dependency parsing, *Proc. of the Computational Natural Language Learning Shared Task Session of the 2007 Joint Conference on Empirical Methods in Natural Language Processing and Computational Natural Language Learning*, 2007.

Nivre, Joakim, De Marneffe, Marie-Catherine, Ginter, Filip, Goldberg, Yoav, Hajic, Jan, Manning, Christopher D., McDonald, Ryan T., Petrov, Slav, Pyysalo, Sampo, Silveira, Natalia, Tsarfaty, Reut, and Zeman, Daniel, Universal dependencies v1: A multilingual treebank collection, *Proc. of the International Conference on Language Resources and Evaluation*, 2016. 52

Noreen, Eric W., *Computer Intensive Methods for Hypothesis Testing: An Introduction*, Wiley, New York, 1989. 19, 21

Open Science Collaboration, An open, large-scale, collaborative effort to estimate the reproducibility of psychological science, *Perspectives on Psychological Science*, 7(6):657–660, 2012. DOI: 10.1177/1745691612462588. 51

Ó Séaghdha, Diarmuid and Korhonen, Anna, Probabilistic distributional semantics, *Computational Linguistics*, 40(3):587–631, 2014. DOI: 10.1162/COLI_a_00194. 54

Ouchi, Hiroki, Shindo, Hiroyuki, and Matsumoto, Yuji, Neural modeling of multi-predicate interactions for Japanese predicate argument structure analysis, *Proc. of the Association for Computational Linguistics*, 2017. DOI: 10.18653/v1/p17-1146. 21

Patil, Prasad, Peng, Roger D., and Leek, Jeffrey, A statistical definition for reproducibility and replicability, *BioRxiv*, 2016. DOI: 10.1101/066803. xiv, 2, 52

Papineni, Kishore, Roukos, Salim, Ward, Todd, and Zhu, Wei-Jing, BLEU: A method for automatic evaluation of machine translation, *Proc. of the Association for Computational Linguistics*, 2002. DOI: 10.3115/1073083.1073135. 4, 27, 31

Peng, Roger D., Reproducible research in computational science, *Science*, 334(6060):1226–1227, 2011. DOI: 10.1126/science.1213847. 52

Peng, Haoruo, Khashabi, Daniel, and Roth, Dan, Solving hard coreference problems, *Proc. of the North American Chapter of the Association for Computational Linguistics*, pages 809–819, 2015. DOI: 10.3115/v1/n15-1082. 26

Petrov, Slav and McDonald, Ryan, Overview of the 2012 shared task on parsing the Web, *Notes of the First Workshop on Syntactic Analysis of Non-Canonical Language*, 2012. 52, 54

Pinter, Yuval, Guthrie, Robert, and Eisenstein, Jacob, Mimicking word embeddings using subword RNNs, *Proc. of the Conference on Empirical Methods in Natural Language Processing*, 2017. DOI: 10.18653/v1/d17-1010. 65

Pennington, Jeffrey, Socher, Richard, and Manning, Christopher, GloVe: Global vectors for word representation, *Proc. of the Conference on Empirical Methods in Natural Language Processing*, 2014. DOI: 10.3115/v1/d14-1162. 54, 66

Plank, Barbara, Søgaard, Anders, and Goldberg, Yoav, Multilingual part-of-speech tagging with bidirectional long short-term memory models and auxiliary loss, *Proc. of the Association for Computational Linguistics*, 2016. DOI: 10.18653/v1/p16-2067.

Pradhan, Sameer, Moschitti, Alessandro, Xue, Nianwen, Ng, Hwee Tou, Björkelund, Anders, Uryupina, Olga, Zhang, Yuchen, and Zhong, Zhi, Towards robust linguistic analysis using OntoNotes, *Proc. of the Special Interest Group on Natural Language Learning Conference on Computational Natural Language Learning*, 2013. 65

Preoţiuc-Pietro, Daniel, Liu, Ye, Hopkins, Daniel, and Ungar, Lyle, Beyond binary labels: Political ideology prediction of twitter users, *Proc. of the 55th Annual Meeting of the Association for Computational Linguistics*, 1:729–740, 2017. DOI: 10.18653/v1/p17-1068. 14

Radinsky, Kira, Agichtein, Eugene, Gabrilovich, Evgeniy, and Markovitch, Shaul, A word at a time: Computing word relatedness using temporal semantic analysis, *Proc. of the International World Wide Web Conference*, 2011. DOI: 10.1145/1963405.1963455. 66

Rastogi, Pushpendre, Van Durme, Benjamin, and Arora, Raman, Multiview LSA: Representation learning via generalized CCA, *Proc. of the North American Chapter of the Association for Computational Linguistics*, 2015. DOI: 10.3115/v1/n15-1058.

Reimers, Nils and Gurevych, Iryna, Reporting score distributions makes a difference: Performance study of LSTM-networks for sequence tagging, *Proc. of the Conference on Empirical Methods in Natural Language Processing*, pages 338–348, 2017. DOI: 10.18653/v1/d17-1035. 45

Reimers, Nils and Gurevych, Iryna, Optimal hyperparameters for deep LSTM-networks for sequence labeling tasks, *ArXiv Preprint ArXiv:1707.06799*, 2017. 45, 47

Reimers, Nils and Gurevych, Iryna, Why comparing single performance scores does not allow to draw conclusions about machine learning approaches, *ArXiv Preprint ArXiv:1803.09578*, 2018. 38, 40, 41, 45

Riezler, Stefan and Maxwell, John T., On some pitfalls in automatic evaluation and significance testing for MT, *Proc. of the Association for Computational Linguistics Workshop on Intrinsic and Extrinsic Evaluation Measures for Machine Translation and/or Summarization*, 2005. 20, 29

Ritter, Alan, Clark, Sam, Mausam, and Etzioni, Oren, Named entity recognition in tweets: An experimental study, *Proc. of the Conference on Empirical Methods in Natural Language Processing*, pages 1524–1534, 2011. 35

Rubenstein, Herbert and Goodenough, John B., Contextual correlates of synonymy, *Communications of the Association for Computing Machinery*, 8(10):627–633, 1965. DOI: 10.1145/365628.365657. 66

Rush, Alexander, Reichart, Roi, Collins, Michael, and Globerson, Amir, Improved parsing and POS tagging using inter-sentence consistency constraints, *Proc. of the Joint Conference on Empirical Methods in Natural Language Processing and Computational Natural Language Learning*, 2012. 18

Sang, Erik F. and Buchholz, Sabine, Introduction to the CoNLL-2000 shared task: Chunking, *4th Conference on Computational Natural Language Learning and the 2nd Learning Language in Logic Workshop*, 2000. DOI: 10.3115/1117601.1117631. 45

Sang, Erik F. and De Meulder, Fien, Introduction to the CoNLL-2003 shared task: Language-independent named entity recognition, *ArXiv Preprint cs/0306050*, 2003. DOI: 10.3115/1119176.1119195. 45

Schuster, Mike and Paliwal, Kuldip K., Bidirectional recurrent neural networks, *IEEE Transactions on Signal Processing*, 45(11):2673–2681, 1997. DOI: 10.1109/78.650093. 35

Schwartz, Roy, Reichart, Roi, and Rappoport, Ari, Symmetric pattern based word embeddings for improved word similarity prediction, *Proc. of the Special Interest Group on Natural Language Learning Conference on Computational Natural Language Learning*, 2015. DOI: 10.18653/v1/k15-1026. 54

Sethuraman, J., The advanced theory of statistics, volume 2: Inference and relationship, *JSTOR*, 1963. 14

Shaked, Moshe and Shanthikumar, J. George, *Stochastic Orders*, Springer Science & Business Media, 2007. DOI: 10.1007/978-0-387-34675-5.

Shapiro, Samuel Sanford and Wilk, Martin B., An analysis of variance test for normality (complete samples), *Biometrika*, 52(3/4):591–611, 1965. DOI: 10.1093/biomet/52.3-4.591. 11

Šidák, Zbyněk, Rectangular confidence regions for the means of multivariate normal distributions, *Journal of the American Statistical Association*, 62(318):626–633, 1967. DOI: 10.2307/2283989. 62

Silberer, Carina, Ferrari, Vittorio, and Lapata, Mirella, Models of semantic representation with visual attributes, *Proc. of the Association for Computational Linguistics*, 2013.

Silberer, Carina and Lapata, Mirella, Learning grounded meaning representations with autoencoders, *Proc. of the Association for Computational Linguistics*, 2014. DOI: 10.3115/v1/p14-1068. 54

Simes, R. John, An improved Bonferroni procedure for multiple tests of significance, *Biometrika*, pages 751–754, 1986. DOI: 10.1093/biomet/73.3.751. 76

Smucker, Mark D., Allan, James, and Carterette, Ben, A comparison of statistical significance tests for information retrieval evaluation, *Proc. of the International Conference on Information and Knowledge Management*, 2007. DOI: 10.1145/1321440.1321528.

Snow, Rion, O'Connor, Brendan, Jurafsky, Daniel, and Ng, Andrew Y., Cheap and fast—but is it good?: Evaluating non-expert annotations for natural language tasks, *Proc. of the Conference on Empirical Methods in Natural Language Processing*, 2008. DOI: 10.3115/1613715.1613751. 54

Srivastava, Nitish, Hinton, Geoffrey, Krizhevsky, Alex, Sutskever, Ilya, and Salakhutdinov, Ruslan, Dropout: A simple way to prevent neural networks from overfitting, *The Journal of Machine Learning Research*, 15(1):1929–1958, 2014. 35

Steiger, James H., Tests for comparing elements of a correlation matrix, *Psychological Bulletin*, 87(2):245–251, 1980. DOI: 10.1037/0033-2909.87.2.245. 67

Søgaard, Anders, Estimating effect size across datasets, *Proc. of the North American Chapter of the Association for Computational Linguistics*, 2013. 19, 55

Søgaard, Anders, Johannsen, Anders, Plank, Barbara, Hovy, Dirk, and Alonso, Héctor Martínez, What's in a p-value in NLP?, *Proc. of the Special Interest Group on Natural Language Learning Conference on Computational Natural Language Learning*, 2014. DOI: 10.3115/v1/w14-1601. 19, 55, 66

Toutanova, Kristina, Klein, Dan, Manning, Christopher D., and Singer, Yoram, Feature-rich part-of-speech tagging with a cyclic dependency network, *Proc. of the Conference of the North American Chapter of the Association for Computational Linguistics on Human Language Technology*, 1:173–180, 2003. DOI: 10.3115/1073445.1073478. 35

Walker, Christopher, Strassel, Stephanie, Medero, Julie, and Maeda, Kazuaki, Semeval-2013 task 1: Tempeval-3: Evaluating time expressions, events, and temporal relations, *2nd Joint Conference on Lexical and Computational Semantics, Volume 2: Proc. of the 7th International Workshop on Semantic Evaluation*, 2:1–9, 2013. 45

Vaswani, Ashish, Shazeer, Noam, Parmar, Niki, Uszkoreit, Jakob, Jones, Llion, Gomez, Aidan N., Kaiser, Łukasz, and Polosukhin, Illia, Attention is all you need, *Advances in Neural Information Processing Systems*, pages 5998–6008, 2017. 35

Vedantam, Ramakrishna, Lawrence Zitnick, C., and Parikh, Devi, Cider: Consensus-based image description evaluation, *Proc. of the IEEE conference on Computer Vision and Pattern Recognition*, pages 4566–4575, 2015. DOI: 10.1109/cvpr.2015.7299087. 31

Vilain, Marc, Burger, John, Aberdeen, John, Connolly, Dennis, and Hirschman, Lynette, A model-theoretic coreference scoring scheme, *Proc. of the 6th Conference on Message Understanding*, pages 45–52, 1995. DOI: 10.3115/1072399.1072405.

Vogel, Curtis R., Computational methods for inverse problems, *Society of Industrial and Applied Mathematics*, 23, 2002. DOI: 10.1137/1.9780898717570.

Walker, Christopher, Strassel, Stephanie, Medero, Julie, and Maeda, Kazuaki, ACE 2005 multilingual training corpus, *Linguistic Data Consortium, Philadelphia*, 57, 2006. 45

Weischedel, Ralph, Hovy, Eduard, Marcus, Mitchell, Palmer, Martha, Belvin, Robert, Pradhan, Sameer, Ramshaw, Lance, and Xue, Nianwen, OntoNotes: A large training corpus for enhanced processing, *Handbook of Natural Language Processing and Machine Translation*, Springer, 2011. 65

Welch, Bernard L., The generalization of students' problem when several different population variances are involved, *Biometrika*, 34(1/2):28–35, 1947. DOI: 10.2307/2332510. 38

Wieting, John, Bansal, Mohit, Gimpel, Kevin, and Livescu, Karen, Towards universal paraphrastic sentence embeddings, *Proc. of the International Conference on Learning Representations*, 2016. 54

Wieting, John and Gimpel, Kevin, Revisiting recurrent networks for paraphrastic sentence embeddings, *ArXiv Preprint ArXiv:1705.00364*, 2017. DOI: 10.18653/v1/p17-1190. 16

Wilcoxon, Frank, Individual comparisons by ranking methods, *Biometrics Bulletin*, 1(6):80–83, 1945. DOI: 10.2307/3001968. 19, 66

Wu, Shuangzhi, Zhang, Dongdong, Yang, Nan, Li, Mu, and Zhou, Ming, Sequence-to-dependency neural machine translation, *Proc. of the Association for Computational Linguistics*, 2017. DOI: 10.18653/v1/p17-1065. 21

Yadav, Vikas and Bethard, Steven, A survey on recent advances in named entity recognition from deep learning models, *Proc. of the 27th International Conference on Computational Linguistics*, pages 2145–2158, 2018. 35

Yang, Bishan and Mitchell, Tom, Leveraging knowledge bases in LSTMs for improving machine reading, *Proc. of the Association for Computational Linguistics*, 2017. DOI: 10.18653/v1/p17-1132. 19

Yang, Dongqiang and Powers, David M. W., Verb similarity on the taxonomy of WordNet, *Proc. of the 3rd International WordNet Conference*, 2006. 66

Yeh, Alexander, More accurate tests for the statistical significance of result differences, *Proc. of the International Conference on Computational Linguistics*, 2000. DOI: 10.3115/992730.992783. 13, 14, 29, 32, 66

Zeiler, Matthew D., ADADELTA: An adaptive learning rate method, *ArXiv Preprint ArXiv:1212.5701*, 2012.

Ziser, Yftah and Reichart, Roi, Neural structural correspondence learning for domain adaptation, *Proc. of the Special Interest Group on Natural Language Learning Conference on Computational Natural Language Learning*, 2017. DOI: 10.18653/v1/k17-1040. 18, 65, 66, 70

Authors' Biographies

ROTEM DROR

Rotem Dror is a Ph.D. student in the Natural Language Processing Research Group under the supervision of Professor Roi Reichart at the Technion, Israel Institute of Technology. Rotem's research interests lie in the intersection of Machine Learning, Statistics, Optimization, and Natural Language Processing. In her Ph.D., she focuses mainly on developing statistical methods for evaluating results of NLP tasks and on novel algorithms for structured prediction in NLP. Rotem's papers have been published in the top-tier conferences and journals of the NLP community. Rotem is a recipient of the Google Ph.D. Fellowship 2018.

LOTEM PELED-COHEN

Lotem Peled-Cohen holds an M.Sc. in Natural Language Processing (cum laude) from the Technion, under the supervision of Professor Roi Reichart. Lotem's research revolved around textual sarcasm, and her work about sarcasm interpretation using monolingual Machine Translation was published in the ACL 2017 Proceedings and appeared in multiple media channels. After her studies, Lotem worked as a Data Scientist, focusing mostly on Conversational AI. She later became an independent consultant and lecturer at ML, NLP, and Deep Learning. Lotem was a lecturer at multiple colleges and presented in conferences worldwide. Nowadays, Lotem brings her ML & NLP expertise to the world of product management at Samsung Next, as part of the Whisk product department. Lotem works as an ML Product Manager who leads a collaboration between Samsung offices worldwide (Korea, Russia, US, and Israel) responsible for building innovative, intelligent, and trustworthy ML products.

SEGEV SHLOMOV

Segev Shlomov is a Ph.D. student under the supervision of Associate Professor Yakov Babichenko at the Technion, Israel Institute of Technology. Segev's research interests lie at the intersection of Statistics, Social Learning, and Information Theory. Segev holds an M.Sc. in Operations Research (summa cum laude) from the Technion. He was three-time a summer intern at the Artificial Intelligence department of the IBM research labs, Haifa, Israel, and he is one of the main contributors to IBM's Lambada AI service. Segev's papers have been published in top-tier conferences and journals of both the NLP community and the Economics and

Computation communities. Segev is a recipient of the Jacobs Outstanding Ph.D. Scholarship for the year 2020.

ROI REICHART

Roi Reichart is an Associate Professor at the Technion, Israel Institute of Technology. Before joining the Technion, on July 2013, he was a post-doctoral researcher at the Computer Laboratory of the University of Cambridge, UK, and at the Computer Science and Artificial Intelligence Laboratory (CSAIL) of MIT. Prior to this, he was a Ph.D. student under the supervision of Professor Ari Rappoport at the Interdisciplinary Center for Neural Computation (ICNC) of Hebrew University of Jerusalem. His main research interest is NLP, with a focus on language learning in its context and designing models that integrate domain and world knowledge with data-driven methods. He has hence worked on problems such as domain adaptation, learning with minimal human annotation (and involvement), language transfer and multilingual learning, multi-modal (text and vision) processing, and NLP of Web data. He has focused on structured aspects of language and has developed effective algorithms for inference across linguistic structures. Finally, he is interested in proper evaluation of NLP algorithms and has worked on problems such as measuring statistical significance in NLP, word embedding evaluation, and unsupervised learning (particularly clustering) evaluation.

Printed in the United States
by Baker & Taylor Publisher Services